"Bishop Neil Ellis' ministry has brought freedom and victory in the lives of hundred of thousands of people around the world. The word that God put in his mouth in this insightful book will encourage you, bless you and challenge you to Pursue God's Glory!"

Pastor John K. Jenkins, Sr.
First Baptist Church of Glenarden, Maryland

"I don't know if it's ever been said more clearly than by Bishop Ellis in Pursuing the Glory: 'Be a candidate for the miraculous to unfold.' In this book, the man of God gives readers another way to look at life's trials. He also explores the tremendous weight of God's glory. Get this book, and find out how to position yourself for the miraculous. It's a great, great read!"

Bishop Eddie L. Long, D.D., D.H.L.
New Birth Missionary Baptist Church
Lithonia, Georgia

"In the summer of 2007 at the Full Gospel Baptist Church Fellowship International Conference it was evident that Bishop Neil C. Ellis was given a divine and urgent mandate for the people of God. As he spoke just above a whisper after being on voice rest from recent surgery on his vocal cords he fervently spoke about a new wave of Glory and it was apparent the glory of God dwelled in the place. If you want to witness the miraculous in your life then this book is for you. I am confident after reading this book your life will never be the same. I encourage you to read each page with expectation of receiving the essence of what we were created for… His glory!"

Bishop Paul S. Morton, Sr., Presiding Bishop,
Full Gospel Baptist Church Fellowship International
New Orleans, Louisianna

"Every now and then God raises up someone with a fresh word, a fresh revelation. Bishop Neil Ellis gives to us a message from the very heart of God. His time of quietness and reflection has provided us with a road map to an intimate and empowering life with God. This is a most read for every believer who is seeking to be used by God."

Bishop Walter S. Thomas
Presiding Prelate Kingdom Association of Covenant Pastors
Pastor New Psalmist Baptist Church
Baltimore, Maryland

"Bishop Neil Ellis is an instrument of revelation. God uses him as an usher who guides us not only into the experience of the glory of God but deeper in knowledge of the God of glory."

Bishop Kenneth Ulmer
Faithful Central Bible Church
Los Angeles, California

"Pursuing the Glory reveals the crucial keys to attaining the total blessing of God's glory in your life – a glory that positions the believer for the pinnacle of destiny our Master Designer has planned for each of us."

Pastor Paula White
Without Walls International Church
Tampa, Florida

In an hour when words are so carelessly misspoken, it is refreshing to read a manuscript penned by a man with such an apostolic mandate.
His unwavering faith during periods of uncertainty has processed, purposed, and promoted him to bring divine distinction and direction to the body of Christ. In this timeless literary charge, "Pursing The Glory", he sets a course of navigational destiny that will guide you into the very presence of God. He is an apostolic father, a co-laborer, and a friend…he is Bishop Neil C. Ellis

Bishop Joby Brady, Founder
River Fellowship International
Durhan, North Carolina

PURSUING THE GLORY

Neil C. Ellis

Pursuing the Glory

Pneuma Life Publishing
12138 Central Ave
Mitchellville, MD 20721
www.pneumalife.com
For bulk purchases call: 1-800-727-3218

Manufactured in the United States of America
10 9 8 7 6 5 4 3 2 1

Paperback   ISBN 10: 1-56229-951-4
ISBN 13: 978-1-56229-951-4

Hardcover   ISBN 10: 1-56229-952-2
ISBN 13: 978-1-56229-952-1

Neil Ellis Ministries
E-mail: info@neilellisministries.com

Bahamas Address
Mt. Tabor Drive
P.O. Box N-9705
Nassau, Bahamas
1-242-392-0708

USA Address
3405 N.W. 189th St.
Miami Gardens, FL 33056-2907
Toll Free 1 (888) 700-FIRE

Dedication

This book is dedicated to the following:

- My faithful and devoted wife of more than 25 years who has taught me how to live and how to love. Patrice has become my greatest 'fan' and continues to be a personal source of encouragement and inspiration.

- To my children, Ranechea and Johnathan whose growth and maturity continue to be a vehicle of strength and determination.

- To the Leadership and Membership of the Mount Tabor Full Gospel Baptist Church whose inspiration has given me impetus to dare such a study and who have shown more interest in my preaching and teaching of the word of God than I have had any right to hope for.

Contents

Foreword

By Paula White

As our world experiences great changes and upheaval, the body of Christ is being called to prepare itself for God's ultimate will to be done on earth. Bishop Neil Ellis is a great general of the faith and prophetic voice delivering God's messages for equipping His people for the next age – and his powerful book, Pursuing the Glory is a vital guide to positioning oneself for God's greatness.

The body of Christ is in crucial times; we are in an age where we cannot afford to miss any opportunity to "hear God" – even as we experience life's tests and trials. While many times our first instinct is to "react" to stressful, challenging, or difficult situations with fear and panic, Pursuing the Glory encourages believers to recognize how unforeseen trials can offer us periods of reflection and a cease from the "norm" – often becoming the very circumstances by which God can, as Bishop Ellis writes, "download from His mind to our mind."

Pursuing the Glory does not shirk from addressing the very real and practical issues many Christians are experiencing these days – rather, Bishop Ellis offers life-transforming insight on how we can change our perspective to find the hand of God at work in all of our circumstances. Through detailed examination and practical application, Bishop Ellis reveals how believers can draw closer to God during the coming period, and experience the kind of miraculous power and deliverance that results from consciously seeking to experience His glory.

As Bishop Ellis prophesies of a coming "collision" between the heavenly realm and the earthly realm, he provides insightful information on how Christians can invite God to abide intimately in their lives – that they might become the very "temples" of His Holy Spirit, written of in 1 Corinthians 6:19. It is this completely encompassing, physically palpable, manifested presence of God that we all desperately need today.

Pursuing the Glory reveals the crucial keys to attaining the total blessing of God's glory in your life – a glory that positions the believer for the pinnacle of destiny our Master Designer has planned for each of us. Bishop Ellis examines numerous Scripture verses alluding to the "glory," exploring its deeper significance in each context. His insightful common-sense approach provides believers with comprehensive, practical, and useful strategies for understanding and seeking God's glory.

Bishop Ellis takes it a step further, revealing how experiencing the glory isn't isolated to a church experience, or a matter of being in the right place at the right time. He reveals how it's possible to call God's glory down upon you with your praise, preparation, and purpose! What good news it is to know we can have full access to God's awesome presence in our lives by preparing a place for Him to abide with us!

Pursuing The Glory ultimately reminds us that it is our responsibility, as God's children, to take seriously the authority He has given us to seek, find, and embody His glory on the earth today. Bishop's Ellis' book will encourage you to become bolder in your worship, inspire you to praise the Lord with a stronger voice, and fill you with a joyous confidence in your relationship with the Father as a child of God.

Bishop Ellis reminds us that the time is now...to walk in the healing, prosperity, faith, courage, determination -- and above all, the love -- that will display to the world the glory and awesome power of our God. So get ready to be refreshed in the spirit by the life-changing revelation that awaits you -- as you embark on the journey to Pursuing The Glory!

Acknowledgement

This work is a result of my personal encounter with God during one of the most critical times in my life and ministry. I am eternally grateful to God for His Divine impartation and revelation which now enables me to be a 'carrier' of this timeless truth.

The Publisher at Pneuma Life, Devin Stewart, and his team of Editors have worked closely with me through this process and I certainly want to acknowledge and thank them.

I also wish to acknowledge my Agent and Personal Consultant DJ Roker who continues to provide assistance and direction to me and "the TEAM" as we seek to carry both the message and the Spirit of the Glory of God around the world.

My Editorial and Marketing Team inclusive of Michelle Duffie, Miranda Inniss, Illsa Evans, Maxine Newton, Grafton Ifill and Pastor Delton Ellis are all worthy of mention and commendation.

Thank you all and to God be the Glory!

Introduction

"For the earth will be filled with the knowledge of the glory of the LORD, as the waters cover the sea." (Habakkuk 2:14)

Over the years, I have had the privilege of blessing many of God's people through my preaching and teaching ministry. So often, people may have heard me speaking in a public place and without hesitation would rush over to me and ask, "Are you Bishop Ellis?" As a preacher, my voice is what a paint brush is to a skilled painter. Often I give thanks to God for giving me this glorious opportunity to open my mouth and use my vocal cords to express how great He is in the earth. *"For the gifts and the calling of God are without repentance."* (Romans 11:29)

In May of 2007, I had to undergo vocal cord surgery to repair a damaged cord in my throat. If you want to put the fear of God in a preacher, take away his ability to speak. Before I had this nerve-racking surgery, I experienced a terrible case of acid reflux disease, caused primarily from late night eating. I had no idea that for years I was damaging my body and that one day I would need major surgery to fix the problem. But, what the devil means for evil, God will turn it around for your good. The Bible lets us know that Jesus was led into the desert to be tempted by the devil. The Holy Spirit must put the squeeze on us if the glory of God is to be realized in our lives.

After the first of three surgeries, there was an eight-week recuperation period. During the first two weeks of recuperation, I was advised not to use my voice at all. What a difficult instruction for a preacher to follow. During this time, I started to lose my mind. I was so frustrated with the process that I ended up putting God on the witness stand. While I was questioning God about what was happening, He reminded me that He had everything under control. The first two weeks after the surgery were the most difficult and frustrating. What I thought was an attack from the enemy was a divine setup by God. God knows what you need when you need it. Adam fell asleep and God brought forth a woman from his side. Sometimes God will put us in a position of being silent so that He can download from His mind into our minds. I needed to hear and receive from God without interrupting Him with my big mouth.

My spirit finally settled, and I was able to manage my time and rest in the peace of God. There was no pain whatsoever, just silence. Did you get that? No pain, just silence. During what I call my season of divine setup by God, I was able to prepare 42 sermons and complete my tenth book, The Power of Pain. During my eight weeks of recovery, the Holy Spirit continued downloading the direction and purpose that He had for my life and the life of the church. God said to me, "When I raise you up and release you to return to the pulpit, I want you to lead the way in restoring My glory back into the church."

I returned to the pulpit the first week in July. As I stood in the space that was so very familiar to me, I looked out and saw faces that I had seen for years, Sunday after Sunday, but this time something was different. Before I could open my mouth, a wave of glory swept over the Body of Christ. While

I was standing in the pulpit, I received a vision from the Holy Spirit and God said, "The whole earth is being prepared to be filled with My knowledge and My glory," just as the Prophet Habakkuk indicated thousands of years ago.

There is soon to be a collision between the heavenly realm and the earthly realm. The barrier that has separated the two realms is being destroyed. Get ready, because the manifested presence of God will be revealed in the earthly realm like never before. I sincerely believe that the information on the pages that follow will provide tremendous assistance in preparing you for what is to come. My friend, it is time to "PURSUE THE GLORY!"

CHAPTER 1

An Environment For The Miraculous

THE PLACE WHERE GOD DWELLS

This is Glory Time! This is the time that you have to let God be God in your life. Where there is glory, God dwells. God dwells in the environment that invokes the glory. If you want to see miracles, signs and wonders manifested in your midst, if you want to see God be God in your life, if you want to see the promises of God unfold right before your eyes, you must continually live with the glory. Living with the glory creates an environment for the miraculous to materialize in your life.

But what does it mean to "live with the glory?" When you live with the glory, the presence of God dominates your life. You are consciously aware of the manifold presence and power of God. You are always around God, God is always around you, and the presence of God controls your every move. When life throws you a curve ball and you think that somehow you have stepped out of His presence, you feel lost and you are desperate to return. But when you live with the glory, every fiber of your being longs for the presence of God. When you live with the glory of God, no matter what is happening in the natural, it is an environment for the miraculous to take place.

Living with the glory means that any day, every day, everywhere, any time, you are a candidate for the miraculous to unfold. God does not ask your permission to give you a miracle. It is God's desire for the body of Christ, individually, as well as collectively, to be the abiding place for His presence. As Christians, as temples of the living God, as keepers of the faith, it is God's desire that our bodies become an abiding place for His presence. Can you imagine all of us coming together in the house of God, each one consciously aware that he is carrying the presence of God? Can you imagine the explosion that would take place every time we get together? My God, only those who can fully understand and appreciate the power of living with the glory can relate to this experience.

Dismantle the mindset that God has anointed only one person in the church who has the ability to flow under the awesome anointing and power of God. God does not operate like that. God is a God of order. He rarely talks to the crowd. He will choose one person out the group to be the leader, and that is the one who will give direction and instruction. God speaks to His leaders and then sends them back to the people to deliver His instructions. However, that does not mean that everyone else is exempt from the anointing of God. Every believer is charged with the responsibility of carrying the glory of God.

Your body is designed to be the temple of the living God, the abiding place of His presence, qualifying you as a carrier of God's Glory. When you fully embrace that divine mandate, your perspective on the things of God, His power, authority, presence and glory will change. You will realize that wherever you go, you carry the glory of God. Because you are carrying the presence of God (or the Glory of God), wherever you are, you are in an environment conducive for the miraculous.

THE WEIGHT OF HIS GLORY

Challenges create a birthing ground for the miraculous to flow and for God's glory to be revealed. When you live with the glory and you are consciously aware of God's presence, challenges no longer intimidate you. They no longer cause you to run and hide. Challenges no longer cause you to back into a corner, overwhelmed and shaking with fear. The weight of the challenge does not compare to the weight of God's glory or the weight of your purposeful worship and adoration of the true and living God who dwells within you. When you are faced with life's difficult challenges, you must lift up your head and give God glory because it is an indication that God wants to work a miracle in your life.

"Lift up your heads, O ye gates; and be ye lifted up, ye everlasting doors; and the King of glory shall come in. Who is this King of glory? The LORD strong and mighty, the LORD mighty in battle." (Psalm 24:7-8)

Perspective is everything. You should not look at your challenges and agree with the difficulty that surrounds them. Don't say, "Well, I have this challenge now because Satan is cursing me. The enemy is attacking my life." No! Just because the devil attacks you, does not mean that you should surrender and allow it to wreak havoc in your life. No! Look at the attack and say, "I am in an environment that is conducive for the miraculous. Lord, how are you going to fix this?"

You have to begin to view attacks and challenges differently. How would God perform miracles if you did not have a need that was beyond your control? Any situation that you can fix on your own is not eligible for a miracle. God only steps in with miracles when you are in a situation that is outside of your total control. If you are dealing with something in your life right now that is outside of your control, you are a candidate for a miracle.

Remember, the weight of the challenge does not compare to the weight of His glory. God's glory can come upon you so quickly that the devil can trick you into believing that you are tired. But it is not a bad thing. It is honorable. Some people experience glory and others experience the weight of glory. Isaiah 60:1-2 says, "Arise, shine; for thy light is come, and the glory of the LORD is risen upon thee. For, behold, the darkness shall cover the earth, and gross darkness the people: but the LORD shall arise upon thee, and his glory shall be seen upon thee."

When you begin to feel the weight of His glory, it is God saying, "Do not be deceived into believing that your physical body is tired. I have placed Myself upon you." It is God beckoning you to rise and shine for your light has come and the glory of the Lord has been placed upon you. So, when the weight of His glory is upon you, God wants you to get up! Don't sit there and succumb to the pressure. Don't sit there and complain. Don't sit there and be depressed. RISE! God's glory is on you!

After the first real wave of glory hit our church one Sunday, as a husband, if I had not perceived the voice of God and understood God's glory, I would have responded ignorantly toward my wife's actions. The following Saturday, my wife, could hardly get out of bed. I could not detect anything wrong with her. At 2:00 p.m. on Saturday afternoon, she was still in bed. So, I decided not to disturb her. I checked on her at 4:00 pm and she was still in bed. Finally, about 5:00 p.m., she got up to check on the family, and by 7:00 p.m. she was back in the bed.

Around 8:00 p.m., Saturday night, it finally hit me; the weight of God's glory was upon her. I got up Sunday morning to prepare for service, looked at my wife and refused to wake her. I had to give her body a chance to adjust to the weight of the glory. I have been a pastor for over 20 years, and unless my wife is out of the country or nursing an ailment, she never misses Sunday morning service. However, on this particular Sunday, the weight of glory was so heavy upon her that she did not have enough strength to wake up. When the glory comes you will have to fight for your strength, fight through the weight because nothing is physically wrong with you. It's just the weight of His glory. You have to say to yourself, "Arise, shine; for thy light is come, and the glory of the LORD is risen upon thee…"

The weight of His glory will wear you down, but you have to tell yourself, "Arise! Don't sit here! Your light has come!" You have to command your hands to praise the Lord because when the weight of the glory is on your shoulder, your hands are outstretched and the last thing you want to do is raise your hands. You are not being carnal. You did not backslide. That is the weight of His glory. You have to command your hands to line up with your spirit. Your spirit says, "I can't afford to miss this season" but your flesh would not second the motion. So, you have to command your body to praise the Lord and experience the fullness of His glory. As the glory of the Lord comes upon you, your responsibility to do damage to the kingdom of darkness increases because your light has come.

There are people who never really get a breakthrough in the flesh because they have never had a breakthrough in the Spirit. If you cannot break through the walls that are blocking your spirit from worshipping God, you will never see a breakthrough in the flesh to meet your need. You have to first get a breakthrough in the Spirit before you see your needs supplied. When you get a breakthrough in the Spirit, God will supply all of your needs according to His riches in glory by Christ Jesus. Break through in the Spirit and watch your breakthrough manifest in the flesh.

OPEN YOUR MOUTH

"Give unto the LORD, O ye mighty, give unto the LORD glory and strength. Give unto the LORD the glory due unto his name; worship the LORD in the beauty of holiness. The voice of the LORD is upon the waters: the God of glory thundereth: the LORD is upon many waters." (Psalm 29:1-3)

One translation of "glory" is "a thought, a hunch or a hint." The season of encountering and experiencing God's glory is a difficult season through which to walk. It is one of the most difficult seasons in God to open your mouth and worship Him. *Psalm 29:9 reads, "The voice of the LORD maketh the hinds to calve, and discovereth the forests: and in his temple doth every one speak of his glory."*

Let's go to Psalm 63.

"O God, thou art my God; early will I seek thee: my soul thirsteth for thee, my flesh longeth for thee in a dry and thirsty land, where

no water is; To see thy power and thy glory, so as I have seen thee in
the sanctuary. Because thy lovingkindness is better than life, my lips
shall praise thee. Thus will I bless thee while I live: I will lift up my
hands in thy name. My soul shall be satisfied as with marrow and
fatness; and my mouth shall praise thee with joyful lips…"
(Psalm 63:1-5)

David said, "I have looked for you. I have come to the sanctuary to see your power and to experience your glory." This same David said in Psalm 29:9 that everyone in the temple should speak of God's glory. You must allow your mouth to line up with your intention. Why did David say that everyone in the temple should speak of God's glory? Because, believe it or not, that is what people come to the sanctuary to see and experience. People want to see the power of God and experience His glory. So, when you come in and you say "Glory," you are letting everyone know that you did not come looking for any individual. You did not come to speak what was on your mind. You did not come to talk about your situation. You did not come to the sanctuary to hear the choir sing. You came looking for His glory. If the choir sings and helps you get there, that is great. You should not be depending on the praise team to tickle your fancy and give you a little push. You should not be looking for the choir to cheerlead you into glory. You should come looking for the glory! You should come in expectation of experiencing His glory. If the singers never sing a word and if the musicians never play a note, you should still see Glory. That is why you came into the sanctuary.

"Then they that feared (worshipped) the LORD spake often one to another: and the LORD hearkened, and heard it, and a book of remembrance was written before him for them that feared the LORD, and that thought upon his name." (Malachi 3:16) What did they do? They spoke to one another. This is not a season to be in isolation. This is not a season to be easily offended. This is not a season to say, "She hurt me. I am not talking to her. I don't want anything to do with her." You have not broken through the spirit of religion until you can break through people. If you want to experience another wave of glory, you must get your heart right. Purify your heart so that only God's love exists, because out of the abundance of the heart the mouth speaks. (Luke 6:45).

Malachi 3:16 says, "Then those who worshipped the Lord spoke to one another." Have you ever had someone come to you in church telling you how hurt they are because something you did to them but you had no clue what you did? You wonder, "What in the world are they talking about?" The entire time in service they are upset, holding on to an offense, while you are as free as a bird, praising God like you lost your mind. Every time you shout, they say, "Look at her, she has hurt my feelings, and now she is in here and shouting!" Or someone gets a breakthrough in church and a disgruntled onlooker is shaking their head saying, "Fake! That's why I hate church people. They are all a bunch of fakes!" But, the truth be told, hurting people hurt people.

Some people in our ministry say, "Bishop really doesn't know the spirits of some of these people around him." They are often quick to talk about the people that serve with me. "If only he knew that there are people around him who do not have good intentions..." Whether they are right or wrong that's not my focus, when I come into the sanctuary, I come to experience glory. Sometimes people may be upset with you, and while you are praising and worshipping God, they are stuck in their state of anger. Let me caution you that it is a sin and a shame for you to get stuck in an offense, and the person who you believe is responsible for your dilemma is as free as a bird. That should be a sign! Open up your mouth and scream, "GLORY!"

A few years ago, I had some people within the ministry who caused problems among some of the members. They spread rumors about me and poisoned their minds. Oddly enough, the people who were told the rumors left the ministry but those who spread the rumors are still there. They come every Sunday and they pay their tithes. Those that were 'poisoned' left but those that spread the 'poison' stayed. It's almost like the 'poisoners' said, "I am going to tell you this, but if you are gullible enough to believe it, then go right ahead. But I am not moving."

If people get offended by your actions and you know you have done nothing to offend them, shake the dust off your feet. Don't wait for them to unload all of their complaints, innuendos and misinterpretations upon you. Just say, "Whatever I have done, forgive me, because all I want is for you to see the power and the glory of God."

CHAPTER 2

Understanding
The Glory

FOUNDATION

Exodus 33:16-19 reads, *"For how then will it be known that Your people and I have found grace in Your sight, except You go with us? So we shall be separate, Your people and I, from all the people who are upon the face of the earth."* So the LORD said to Moses, *"I will also do this thing that you have spoken; for you have found grace in My sight, and I know you by name."* And he said, *"Please, show me Your glory."*

Habakkuk 2:14 reads, *"For the earth will be filled with the knowledge of the glory of the LORD, as the waters cover the sea."*

Isaiah 40:4-5 reads, *"The voice of one crying in the wilderness:
'Prepare the way of the LORD; Make straight in the desert
a highway for our God. Every valley shall be exalted and every
mountain and hill brought low; the crooked places shall be made
straight and the rough places smooth; the glory of the LORD shall
be revealed, and all flesh shall see it together; for the mouth of the
LORD has spoken.'"*

These words written by Isaiah resonate in my spirit today.
You are in a season where every valley in your life shall be
exalted; every mountain and hill in your life shall be made low;
the crooked places in your life shall be made straight, and the
rough places in your life shall be made smooth; and yes, the
glory of the Lord SHALL be revealed - not might, not could,
but SHALL be revealed - and all flesh shall see it together, for
the mouth of the Lord has spoken. This is a promise, a mandate,
a proclamation from God. The glory of the Lord SHALL be
revealed. It is not an option. The glory of the Lord shall be
revealed and we shall all see it. Everyone may not bask in the
glory and enjoy His presence but the glory of the Lord shall be
revealed and all flesh shall see it together. We should all desire
to be one of the chosen who will experience His glory and not
sit on the sidelines looking through binoculars and watching
it happen. We have a wonderful opportunity to bask in His
glory and experience the benefits firsthand. However, in order
to experience His glory to the fullest, we must understand the
glory of God.

PRAYER, PRAISE AND WORSHIP

Let me share with you a portion of the vision statement of Mount Tabor Full Gospel Baptist Church.

"It is the firm conviction of the Bishop that the Lord is preparing the Body of Christ for one of the greatest manifestations of His presence in ancient and modern history. Consequently, it is the Bishop's view, that a wave of glory is coming to Mount Tabor, and when it does, it will be big, powerful and it will last for a while. It is the vision of the Bishop therefore, that none in active membership will miss it this time. The Bishop sees a praying, praising, worshipping people who are willing to fight for this fulfillment in their lives."

Not only is a wave of glory coming to the church that I pastor, Mount Tabor Full Gospel Baptist Church but it is coming to the body of Christ in general. In order for us to bask in His glory and experience the benefits firsthand, we must be a people of prayer, praise and worship. We cannot be afraid to pray or ashamed to praise. We cannot be reluctant and hesitant to worship God. The mouth of the Lord has spoken, and yes, a wave of His glory is coming. That is exciting news! We are not just going to see the glory of the Lord; we are going to see a wave of His glory. It's going to be big, it's going to be powerful, and it's going to last for a while. But we must purpose in our hearts to be a praying, praising and worshipping people.

Most people are not reluctant to cheer on their favorite sports team. They are not afraid to let it be known which political party they support. They are not afraid to show their support for their country's Olympic team. Therefore, Christians should not be afraid to pray because prayer is our method of communicating with our God. Prayer is how we talk to God, and through the scriptures God speaks back to us. Prayer encompasses our verbal communication with God and reading the scriptures. Our prayer life is not right because our worship is not right. We come to church looking for a hand out from God - "Bless me, Lord. I am here today." And some of us go as far as to threaten God by saying, "If I don't get a word from God today, I'll give up." This is why the glory must return back to the church, so that our focus will return back to the One who loves us unconditionally. We will talk a little bit more about prayer in a later chapter.

You cannot be ashamed to praise God publicly or privately. You should be able to express your love, adoration, appreciation and reverence of the Most High God to anyone, anywhere. You should be able to declare, "Yes, I love the Lord." You cannot desire God's glory and long to be in His presence, but be ashamed of Him in public because the Glory of God will not necessarily hit you in private. We need more people of God who are not ashamed of the gospel of Jesus Christ, people who are not ashamed to let people know, "I am saved and I'm glad about it."

As a believer in the true and living God, you must come out of the closet. You must come out of hiding. You cannot stay behind the scenes. You must surface and let the world know that you are affiliated with and connected to God. Let the world know, "I am a Christian. I believe in Jesus Christ. I belong to God and He belongs to me." You should not be more vocal about your football team than you are about your Creator and your Redeemer.

Many people attend pageants and cheer for their favorite contestant. We will scream, yell, holler and even have a drink in celebration. Yet many people are not eager to let people know that they are Christians. Members of the Body of Christ who really believe God and love Him with their whole hearts have to be more than just a Christian on Sunday morning. Christianity is a lifestyle. The powerful principles of Jesus Christ must be reflected in your walk and in your talk everyday. Are you saved and not ashamed to tell it? Are you a believer in the true and the living God and not afraid to proclaim His name? Then you cannot be reluctant to praise Him. You cannot be reluctant to worship Him.

You must be prepared to bow down and worship Him in ways of that you are not accustomed. Sometimes God will take you off your legs and put you on your face so that you can reverence Him and hear His voice. You are better off worshipping God voluntarily because there will come a time when He will knock you down to get your attention. Jesus said, "Every knee shall bow and every tongue shall confess that Jesus Christ is Lord, unto the glory of God." I don't just want Him to be Lord; I want Him to be Lord of my life, Lord of my family, Lord of my church and Lord of my home!

ONE GOD!

We have no other God but Jehovah. Our God reigns and He reigns forevermore. He is the King of every king, and He is Lord over every lord. Our God is the great I Am. No one can make me doubt Him because I already know too much about Him. He is El Shaddai. He is Adonai. He is Jehovah Nissi and Jehovah Rophe. He is a bridge over troubled waters. He is bread when I am hungry and water when I am thirsty. Our God reigns forever! If you have any other God, then you are out of order. We serve God Almighty and of this we should never be ashamed.

We cannot want the gifts of God without being prepared to brag about Him and declare how awesome He is. We must stop wanting God's gifts without being prepared to brag about the Gift-Giver. God does not necessarily want you to talk about the gift. He prefers you to brag about Him. We must glorify God because of the many blessings He has given us. Take a moment and glorify Him now with the fruit of your lips. Let your words go up to heaven like a sweet smelling savor. Let God Almighty know that you are grateful.

The heart of God is to draw near to His people, more so than to give them things. *"Seek ye first the kingdom of God and his righteousness and all of these things shall be added unto you."* (Matthew 6:33) The real purpose of the church from God's perspective is to become the place for His abiding presence.

What distinguishes us as the people of God are not the poor that we serve. The Red Cross and other social service agencies serve the poor as well. What distinguishes us as the people of God is not necessarily the number of houses that we build or help people to acquire. The government has many programs to serve that need as well. What distinguishes us as the people of God is not how we come together and sing, shout, clap and dance. People sing, shout, dance and clap in the night clubs; as a matter of fact, they do a better job of that than many Christians. What distinguish us as the people of God are not the religious rituals and behaviors that we practice. Non-Christians kneel and pray; unbelievers find time to pray; and even heathens go to church. However, what does distinguish us as the people of God is that we are the abiding place for the presence of God.

People should know that when they walk into the House of God, they will see God in all of His splendor, in all of His power, and in all of His Glory. Quite frankly, that should be the motivating factor behind coming to church. We do not go to church to hear the choir sing or to watch the praise and worship team. They may help us to get closer to the place where we can experience His presence, His power and His Glory but they should not be the purpose for coming. We do not come to church to tithe. Tithing is an act of obedience that is carried out by believers. We know by now that God does not need our money. God says, "When you come to church don't just come to get something from me. I want you to come with a mindset, first of all, to bring something to me." That is the purpose of the tithe. He first wants to obligate you to commit to 10% of whatever it is that He has blessed you with that week; then He wants to test your ability to trust Him with an offering. Jesus said, "The same measure you give to me will determine the measure that I give back to you." That is why so many believers who tithe are still suffering. They follow the command of God as it relates to what He has obligated them to do but they do not trust Him in the offering.

THIS IS GOD'S HOUSE

Going to church is not about singing, shouting, praying, giving, and tithing, as much as it is about having real, genuine fellowship with God. Going to church really is not a time of comfort for you because that is not its purpose. The church is God's house and He is the one who should be King. He is King of the House. We should always seek to create an environment that is comfortable for God. We should always be uncomfortable because there is a reverence, a holy fear when we talk about trying to get into the presence of God. The church should not be the place to come to relax. It is not your house. You are a guest. The church is only your place of identification. It is your place of meeting, the assigned house in your life where you go to corporately meet the Lord. Don't treat it like it is your house. Go into the house of the Lord like you are a guest.

You don't go to a person's home and pull out a cigarette to smoke. You get permission to smoke. You don't go to a person's home and head straight to their refrigerator. You ask, "May I have a cool drink?" That is the problem with the church today.

People want to come to the Lord's House and do what they want to do. God will not show up in their lives because they display bad manners when they come into His House. You must have a holy fear. You must have a reverence for God. I have concluded that a part of the problem with the today's church is that too many people have lost their fear of God.

Some Christians are comfortable living in sin because they come in the House of God on Sunday without fear. They live in sin without assuming that God could strike them down. Holy reverence for God must return to the House of God.

The Church of the living God has to be deemed once again as holy ground. Unfortunately, some people will come to church and sing, "We are standing on holy ground" without reverence. Some will sing about 'standing on holy ground' and bite their nails at the same time without having true reverence. This is an abomination. There must be a respect for God's House. People must be challenged to go into the House of God acknowledging that it is a privilege just to be in His presence. The old proverb that "familiarity breeds contempt" is true, even in the church.

However, rest assured; there will be a revelation of the glory of God in the church. You can take that to the bank! God's manifested, revealed presence will be experienced as long as there is a remnant of people who are sold out to God and willing to acknowledge that every time they come into the house of God, it is to experience His power and His Glory.

TRUE FELLOWSHIP WITH GOD

God longs for real fellowship with a people He can call His own. We have become so programmed in this society to be a progressive generation that God and godly things are way at the bottom of our list of priorities. Some of us would be much further spiritually if we were still surviving on meager means. What happened in some instances was the opposite of what God expected from us. God's thoughts were, "If I bless her now, she will praise me more." But you are doing less. What else can account for the fact that our parents had a stronger praise and worship without even knowing its name. In the 1950's and '60's, with less instruments, no cushioned pews, no air-condition and no microphones, they worshipped God more sincerely. Can you tell me why they were able to give God more glory than He receives in 2009? We have more things but our outward expression of worship and praise is much less.

Unfortunately, the blessings of the Lord have hurt some of us. Can you tell me why when we had less things, there were less crimes in our communities? Globally, we have become a greedy and ungrateful people. Until the nations turn back to God we will continue to see an increase in crime and other social ills. You can take that as a prophetic word. If the truth be told, the real problem we have in our communities is church people.

We cannot blame the government and social agencies for the global state of affairs. *"If my people, which are called by my name, shall humble themselves, and pray, and seek my face, and turn from their wicked ways; then will I hear from heaven, and will forgive their sin, and will heal their land."* (2 Chronicles 7:14) Everyone wants to be blessed but it is the blessings of God that has many people in the state where they are seemingly unable to give God true worship and experience His glory.

Maybe if God begins to strip some people of their possessions, they would start praying a little more. Let me advise you, "Do not force God's hand." I hear God saying, "If the church does not come back into holy order and reverence and produce people who are known for praising and worshipping God, then our economies will continue to collapse and the little that some have will be taken away and our possessions will be lost."

As a believer in Christ, what is your greatest priority in life? What do you want most in life? If your response is something that you can park in your garage; you have missed the mark. If it is a spouse; you have missed it. If it is something to take to the bank; you are way off course. Your greatest desire in life should be, "Lord, show me your glory." I have offered up Mount Tabor as a candidate in the Bahamas for the glory of God to be revealed, and we will see the manifested presence of God in all of His splendor and His Glory. We must be a people whose greatest priority is seeing the glory of God. My prayer is, "Show me Lord, show me. If you have to take my house, take it; if you have to take all the cars, take them but show me. Don't let me miss what you are doing and saying in this season".

Let God do a deep work in your heart and in your life. For some people, God cannot get into their hearts because too many people are in it. I pray that there will be enough of us around the world that develop a hunger for God and His Glory. As a result of this passion, we will begin to see the Spirit of God flowing out of us like a mighty river and nothing will hinder the manifestation of His glory in our lives.

MANIFESTED GLORY

The Church is getting ready to be infused with a deep sense of God's presence, to the point where some people will not be able to stand in it. The day has come when the Church must pursue God's presence, His power, and His Glory more than anything else. It is a matter of priority for it is only in the glory realm that we will ever find our true destiny and fullness of joy.

Remember, glory occurs when there is a collision between the heavenly realm and the earthly realm. When the barrier between the two realms is removed then God comes out of His realm into our realm, and we experience His presence in a personal way.

Jesus said to His disciples, "When you pray, say, 'Our Father, who art in heaven, hallowed be thy name. Thy kingdom come, thy will be done on earth as it is in heaven.'" (Luke 11:2) Allow me to translate those powerful words of Jesus. "Our Father, who art in heaven, hallowed be thy name. Please step out of your realm into this earth realm, and let me experience you in my life so what is going on in my life matches what is going on in heaven."

Manifested glory is when God's realm supersedes the realm you live in and you experience His glory through one or more of your five natural senses. You don't have to wait to experience His glory because glory occurs in your life when the realm of God supersedes the realm in which you presently live. In other words, glory occurs in your life when the barrier in your life that separates the two realms is removed. God will step into your realm when you totally surrender to Him, saying, "Lord, take over!" That means, let your kingdom come and let your will be done in my life, as it is in heaven. If you have never been to heaven and you have never seen the agenda of heaven, you cannot make what is happening in heaven happen in you. You need someone who knows what is happening in the heavenly realm to step over.

Moses was the leader of the children of Israel. He did not cry out to God, "Show us Your glory." Moses said "Show me Your glory." When Moses saw the burning bush, he witnessed the Lord in a tangible way. The glory of God transcends normalcy. The bush was burning, but it was not consumed. God did not call the group. He said, "Moses, take off your shoes, for the place where you are standing is holy ground." God was saying, "Moses, this is Me. I Am here. Take off your shoes, for the place where you are standing is holy ground."

The first time glory is mentioned in the Old Testament, it is connected to holiness. God's glory is lacking in many of our churches because holiness is absent from the church from the top down. When you publicly acknowledge your call to God, you lose your options. When you accept the call of God on your life and you proclaim to be a mouthpiece of God, you are required to be faithful. You cannot blame people, you cannot be super-sensitive, and you cannot be insecure. It is required of you to be faithful.

Too many people are acknowledging the call of God on their lives for reasons other than commitment, faithfulness and holiness. If you fail to live holy, you will not preach holiness. How will the people hear without a preacher? Congregations all over the world are full of scavengers because holiness is rarely preached from the pulpit. Some preachers are intimidated by their members and are afraid that someone may stand up in the service and say something in disagreement or contrary to the message of holiness. That is why God has to carefully select the places where He manifests His glory.

"But without faith it is impossible to please Him, for he who comes to God must believe that He is, and that He is a rewarder of those who diligently seek Him." (Hebrews 11:6)

Every ministry will not qualify for His glory. God has to carefully look to find those who are worthy to experience His manifested glory. He rewards those who diligently seek Him. Diligence comes with commitment and tenacity. Diligence comes with holiness. You cannot allow fear to overtake you when you are seeking to experience the presence of God. Just know that the presence of God exposes the thieves in the temple.

A CALL FOR HOLINESS

I am calling for preachers throughout the Body of Christ around the world to return to a life of holiness, without which none of us will see God. Turn around and cease from your wicked ways. Stand up as a righteousness instrument and be holy.

No church can effectively carry the glory of God if wickedness, un-holiness and unrighteousness are sitting in the pulpit. When the glory of God is being revealed, every servant must have a pure heart. As the old church mothers and fathers used to say, "It's either holiness or hell." As co-laborers of the gospel, we must be committed to upholding the tenets of holiness and righteousness. We cannot say, "Well, I am only a servant. We have to actively get on board and begin to catapult holiness into the atmosphere. The mothers of the church have to be weeping and wailing, crying out for the glory of God to return to His house.

Every evangelist must cry out, "The wages of sin is death." Your sermons cannot be too nice. You must stand up on the street and proclaim holiness, righteousness and the mandate of living a life that is pleasing unto God. You are supposed to carry with you the fear of the living God. The nations should tremble at the sound of your voice.

Pew members must be committed to living a life of holiness. They must strive for a level of commitment that takes them beyond, singing, praying, praising, shucking, and jiving. That is not a good combination. Unfortunately, we have made the pew members unaccountable. Nevertheless, in this dispensation of God's glory, everyone is responsible. Everyone should participate in ushering in the manifested glory of God into His House.

When the glory comes, you are accountable for ensuring that God does not regret it. You are accountable for ensuring that God does not regret allowing you to experience His manifested presence when the glory illuminates your life. Don't just cry out for His glory because glory does not come cheap. The glory of God is manifested in His character, and when we experience His glory we experience the character of God. The glory of God is also experienced through His power and the very essence of who He is. After careful consideration during eight weeks alone with Him, I decided to offer my congregation to God as a people that He can trust with His glory.

THE ATMOSPHERE OF HEAVEN

Just as air is the atmosphere of earth, glory is the atmosphere of heaven. When the heavenly realm is revealed in the earth, we describe the experience as an encounter with the glory of God. Every moment, unconsciously, we inhale and exhale. We are constantly inhaling oxygen and exhaling carbon dioxide. We don't seek permission to breathe; it is automatic, we just breathe. We don't ask God, "Will you trust me with your breath today?"

So it is with the glory of God, which is the atmosphere of heaven. According to the scriptures, the angels bow down and worship God day and night. No one has to tell them to do it. They do not need prior permission to worship. They just do it instinctively, automatically, on impulse. They just respond to the atmosphere.

Our hearts' desire is for the atmosphere of heaven to invade the atmosphere of earth. However, do you think God will allow His glory to invade the earthly realm before He sees our heart and our commitment to worship Him? Worship is a byproduct of the atmosphere of heaven. If you are not a worshipper, if you do not have the heart of a worshipper (not a yeller or screamer) then you are not going to experience the glory of God.

God is a Spirit: and they that worship him must worship him in spirit and in truth. (John 4:24)

You have to worship God from your spirit. If your spirit does not worship Him, you will never lift your hands in adoration and surrender. Your worship is an outward manifestation of your inward feelings toward God. Some people start running, but you do not have to run to worship Him. Running is just a reaction to what is going on in your spirit. Your spirit is saying, "I command my body to worship Him, then all of a sudden you start running, clapping and lifting your hands. Your spirit commanded your body. That is an indication that your body has now come under subjection.

The glory will cause your mind, body and spirit to come into alignment with the presence of God. Young men will begin to pull up their pants; the smoker will stop smoking; the alcoholic will stop consuming alcohol. The Holy Spirit revealed to me that I should stop preaching on bringing the body into subjection to the Spirit and start preaching on the glory, and the glory will take care of everything else.

There are too many weak people in our pulpits and in our churches. One little pain, one little heartache, and they want God to give them an exemption. When I was ill I had to command my voice to preach. I didn't have any time to worry about my physical challenges. I had to bring my throat under subjection because I knew I had to preach. Likewise, you have to command your hands to praise God. You have to command your mouth to praise Him. You have to command your lips to honor God. Don't go to church and succumb to your body feeling tired. Command your body to over power the spirit of weariness. Put on the garment of praise, and let God be glorified.

When God's manifested presence is revealed, when He shows up in all of His glory, the totality of all that He is and all that He has is present. Everything that God is shows up with His glory, and everything that God has comes along with Him. Sickness cannot survive in the manifested presence of God, because God is a healer. Lack cannot survive in the manifested presence of God, because God is Jehovah Jireh. He is a supplier of all of our needs. The problem is not lack of money or things, the problem is the lack of His glory. Therefore, we must personally cry out, "Lord, show me your glory! Show me your glory."

THE GLORY CLOUD

When the manifested glory of God is present, anything is possible. However, you have to change your mindset. When the glory of God is present, you enter into a realm that supersedes the norm. What was impossible is now possible because of the presence of the living God.

Business owners, while you are corporately waiting and preparing for the glory, allow your mind to consider extension, expansion, development and new product lines. Don't just wait for the glory, prepare for it because when the glory is revealed it is time for action. It is not time for consideration. You must consider in the midst of preparation, on your way to manifestation.

Many single women are in church plotting, planning and trying to devise schemes to find a husband. Get the glory and you won't need to wear low-cut dresses or short hem lines to attract a man. When darkness hits the earth and gross darkness the people, a man who desires a wife will look for someone who has the light. The light will set you apart from everyone else. Get ready! Get ready! Get ready! When the glory comes, all things are possible. There is a rumbling in the heavenlies. God is about to remove the barriers and step in. However, to experience the fullness of His glory, there must be a hunger. Glory is not a feeling. Glory is not the chills. Glory is not the presence of a person. Glory is the presence of Almighty God in our midst.

"And it came to pass, when Moses came down from mount Sinai with the two tables of testimony in Moses' hand, when he came down from the mount, that Moses wish not that the skin of his face shone while he talked with him. And when Aaron and all the children of Israel saw Moses, behold, the skin of his face shone; and they were afraid to come nigh him. And Moses called unto them; and Aaron and all the rulers of the congregation returned unto him: and Moses talked with them.

And afterward all the children of Israel came nigh: and he gave them in commandment all that the LORD had spoken with him in mount Sinai. And till Moses had done speaking with them, he put a vail on his face. But when Moses went in before the LORD to speak with him, he took the vail off, until he came out. And he came out, and spake unto the children of Israel that which he was commanded. And the children of Israel saw the face of Moses, that the skin of Moses' face shone: and Moses put the vail upon his face again, until he went in to speak with him." *(Exodus 34:29-35)*

In Exodus 33, Moses cried out, "Lord, show me your glory," and God promised him that He would. God told Moses, "I will bring my presence, but I will have to hide you in the cleft of the rock and show you my backside." You will not be able to see my face and survive." Moses got a taste of God's glory.

There was great brilliance and glory on Moses. One theologian said, when the people looked in Moses' face it was like the sun was glaring in their eyes. So, Moses had to put on a veil to preach. He had to put on a veil to talk to the people and he only took it off when he went to talk with God. After he was finished talking to God, he put the veil back on and gave the children of Israel the report from God. He could not talk to them without a veil covering his face.

Something happens to you when the glory overtakes you. You may not be noisy, you may not shout, but everyone will see that there is something on you. That is the light to which the Gentiles run. (Isaiah 60).

And believers were the more added to the Lord, multitudes both of men and women. Insomuch that they brought forth the sick into the streets, and laid them on beds and couches, that at the least the shadow of Peter passing by might overshadow some of them. There came also a multitude out of the cities round about unto Jerusalem, bringing sick folks, and them which were vexed with unclean spirits: and they were healed every one. (Acts 5:14-16)

Peter was a carrier of the glory and believers were increasingly added to the church daily. They bought the sick out into the street and laid them on beds and couches, hoping that Peter's shadow might fall on them and they would be healed. The glory on him was so strong that he was not rebuking the enemy or casting out the devil. Peter simply walked by the crowd and the people realized that something was on him. This is the same Peter who denied Jesus yet when he experienced the glory, he changed. There is a difference between who you were before you encountered His glory and who you are after you encounter His glory. It does not matter who you are right now, when the glory hits, there will be a difference.

That is why God told me, "You don't have to preach on sin." He said, "Don't worry about who they are now. If they experience My glory they will change." When the glory comes to the church, you will begin to witness people repenting like never before. Godly sorrow will return to His house. This is no time for fun and games and joking around. The glory is coming and we must be prepared to receive it, experience it and then allow others to be blessed by it.

CHAPTER 3

His Manifested Presence

"The voice of one crying in the wilderness: 'Prepare the way of the LORD; Make straight in the desert a highway for our God. Every valley shall be exalted and every mountain and hill brought low; the crooked places shall be made straight and the rough places smooth; the glory of the LORD shall be revealed, and all flesh shall see it together; for the mouth of the LORD has spoken.'" (Isaiah 40:4-5)

GOD BEYOND

The time is near when the people of God will experience His revealed, manifested presence of God. This is not just a hope. This is not just a desire. This is a reality that will hit us in the face in due season. The Lord showed me that His manifested, revealed presence will show up as a wave and will hit Mount Tabor. However, the wave will be so powerful and so large that it will not be contained in one church. The entire city, the island and country, and ultimately the world will get a taste of glory divine because of His manifested presence.

We must accept the fact that whenever God's people get together in the name of Jesus, He has promised to be in the midst. The question is, will He be in our midst in His omnipresence, or will He be in our midst in His manifested presence? The answer remains and rests squarely on the shoulders of those who have come to worship Him.

If we are simply content, only to meet in the name of Jesus as casual observers and do church as usual then we will experience Him in His omnipresence just like those in bar rooms, courtrooms and jailhouses. They also experience the omnipresence of God. The omnipresence of God is generic. *"Whither shall I go from thy spirit? Or whither shall I flee from thy presence? If I ascend up into heaven, thou art there: if I make my bed in hell, behold, thou art there."* (Psalm 139:7-8)

God is everywhere at the same time, but His manifested presence is not everywhere. You have to be hungry for His manifested presence to be revealed in your life. If we want to see God in all of His power, in all of His splendor, in all of His Glory, then we want to experience His manifested presence. Therefore, we must go beyond, seeing God in His omnipresence where we talk about Him being a roof over our head, food on our table, and clothes on our backs. He clothes the wicked. He feeds the ungodly. Not everyone with a roof over their head loves Jesus.

We must desire to go beyond what is generic. We do not want to know God as just the provider. We want to know Him in the fullness of His presence. We want to be able to sense His revealed manifested presence. We want to be able to taste it and feel it and experience it. Remember, there is more to experiencing God than getting "things" from Him. There is a higher level in God than blessings. There is obedience. And there is a level of surrender that is higher than just receiving a blessing from God.

When you obey God and surrender yourself to Him, you begin to walk with Him and talk with Him. You live with a deep sense of peace and contentment. It does not matter what is going on in your life because you walk with God and you know that He has you covered.

Moses told God, "I know you are saying take the children of Israel to Canaan and you will give them the land that you promised them. You are going to give them everything you promised their forefathers, and you are going to scatter their enemies." When God said to Moses, "I am not going with them, My presence will not be with them because they are a stiff-necked people. However, I cannot break My promise and even though they have been disobedient, I still have to bless them. I promised their fathers and their forefathers that is what I would do for their descendants. Nevertheless, My presence will not go with them." Moses said, "God, if your presence does not go with us, leave us here in the wilderness. We prefer to stay in the wilderness eating manna and drinking water out of a rock and be in your presence, than to go into paradise without You."

Moses' conclusive desire is not very popular among many saints today. They prefer God to give them things rather than to be in His presence. "Just fix me up. You don't have to come, God. I don't want to trouble you. Just give me the house, the car, the husband, the wife, the money, the promotion, and the increase. You don't have to come, God because this is not really about you anyway. Now, if you promise me that you will be in church on Sunday, I will come. But you don't have to leave with me. I don't need you in my daily routine, just give me the health and give me the strength, and I will take it from there."

However, if we are glory seekers we should be saying, "Lord, if you don't go with me, leave me where I am because as long as I am in your presence, I will experience the fullness of joy."

THE REAL PURPOSE OF THE CHURCH

All flesh should die in His presence. You don't go to church to flaunt yourself. You go to church to see His power and experience His glory. If you really want to witness the manifested presence of God, you must be hungry for it. You must have an insatiable appetite for God's presence. God is not going to abide in a place that is not hungry for Him. He desperately wants to draw near to His people but we must hunger and thirst after Him.

The purpose of the church is not to produce a good choir or a good praise team nor is it to have great programs and great ministries. The true purpose of the church, from God's perspective, is to become the place for His abiding presence. In the Old Testament, the church is referred to as the "tabernacle." The word "tabernacle" means, "to sit at rest." We desire God to tabernacle with us. Every time we gather to worship God, our worship should produce an aroma and we should have an encounter that defies explanation. Sadly, however, some of us have become so familiar with God and the worship service that we have made the move of God predictable.

It doesn't take an anointing to have church. All you have to do is be around the church long enough and you can pick up the flow of what happens Sunday after Sunday. Having church has become an art. In five minutes, some pastors can have everyone in church on their feet. They are veterans at having church. They know what to stop and what to start. They know how to sing and when to modulate their voices. They even know how to get the congregation in a groove, and how to get the choir and the musicians to back them. Without any push from God, without any special touch from God, without any kind of fresh anointing, they can manufacture an explosive emotional response from within the congregation that will cause many persons to leave the service saying, "God sure did move!" But did He really?

Subsequently, for the glory of the Lord to be fully understood, it must be experienced; it can never be conjured up or manufactured. It comes when the people of God pray, praise and worship the Almighty and cry out to Him earnestly and consistently for revival then he decides to favor His people with His abiding presence and show them His glory. I have already told the Lord that He can use my church to manifest His glory not only for our good but for our entire world. When we get it, we will bask in it, and we will protect it.

There comes a time in your life when God's realm must supersede the realm in which you are accustomed to living. You are in this world but not of it. Your life should be governed and controlled by the heavenly realm, even though you live on earth. The heavenly realm should control all of your actions and decisions. You can ask God to let you get to the point in your life while you are living on earth that your life is dominated by what is going on in heaven.

PEACE IN THE MIDST OF THE STORM

"We are troubled on every side, yet not distressed; we are perplexed, but not in despair; Persecuted, but not forsaken; cast down, but not destroyed..." (2 Corinthians 4:8-9)

We could be troubled on every hand but not downcast because we know that even though we see what is going on in the earthly realm, it does not govern our lives. We can have peace in the midst of a storm because we are seeing a storm in the earth realm but experiencing peace from the heavenly realm. The peace you are experiencing from the heavenly realm is superseding what you are experiencing in the earth realm. When you live by this principle, people can lie on you and talk about you and you can move on like nothing happened.

If it were not for His glory, many of us would be dead. If it were not for the heavenly realm superseding some of us, we would not have been able to tolerate all the hell in our lives. Despite our daily challenges, long suffering, joy and peace are some of the fruit that enable us to endure. In the midst of tribulation and trials, get to the place where you can turn the other cheek. Let your life be governed by what is going on in the heavenly realm and you will be able to make it in this earthly realm.

You can be knee deep in debt but still be able to enjoy a night of sweet, restful sleep. You don't have to stay up all night worrying and pacing the floor because you are grappling with a difficult situation. The joy of the Lord which comes from the realm of glory saturates and supersedes any trials you face. Weeping may endure for a night but when the joy kicks in, the glory of God takes over! Yes, you will have sorrow; yes, you will have troubles; you will sometimes grapple with sadness and disappointment but your life is governed by the realm of heaven.

WHAT'S THE DIFFERENCE?

When you talk about the glory of God, you are not talking about a feeling. You are talking about the presence of a person.

Glory is the presence of Almighty God in our midst and we are blessed by the privilege of dwelling in His presence. The manifested presence of God is what differentiates the church from the Rotary Club, Red Cross, Toastmasters, and other social organizations. There are many buildings with God's name on them and maybe a cross but when you enter, there is not much that distinguishes them from social clubs. That is why some people settle for having services at home because they don't see anything in the church that sets it a part. On the other hand, some uncommitted people of God prefer to stay home and watch television on Sundays. They ask, "What is the difference?"

What are your friends saying about your church? "Oh, that's the church that is really generous;" "that's the church that helps people;" "they look out for their members;" or "the music is good in that church." Are they saying anything else?

It took vocal cord surgery for me to understand that with all that some of us are doing in Christendom; we are missing the most essential element of God. There are mega churches around the globe that average hundreds and thousands of attendees each week. They are community conscious and have done a lot to feed the hungry, clothe the naked and preserve the name of God in their respective communities. Despite their best efforts, however, sometimes serious accusations are hurled against the church but the question remains, have we been accused of being a church where the presence of God dwells?

God said to me, "Son, stop hurting yourself. Just get the glory in the house and that will take care of the rest. Pastors will not have to preach hard once the glory comes because everyone will fall into proper alignment or the glory of God will make people so miserable that they will fall away. The wave of glory will sweep over churches all around the world with such ferocity in this next season that very often people will never hear the message when they come to the sanctuary. As they walk through the door, they will fall flat on their faces under the power of God before they even get to a pew, and remain in His presence for hours. Others will never make it to the tithe box because on their way, they will drop under the power of God's presence. Those are the kinds of signs and wonders we can expect when the glory comes.

It is impossible for the heavens to open and the presence of God to come into our earthly realm and we assume that God would not take care of His people in the process. After the glory falls, people who have damned you for life will come back to beg your pardon. Therefore, we must adopt a spirit of humility and forgiveness. If we know we have been wronged by people, many of whom are very close relatives and friends, we don't need any tricks or gimmicks to get back at them. All we have to do is get into His presence, experience His glory and God will enter into the situation.

God wants to rule and reign in our lives and in our churches anything on our agenda that does not give Him glory, we must cut off because a wave of glory is about to sweep over the Church.

REWARD IN THE GLORY

Stop going after stuff and go after the glory. If we go after the glory, the "things" will follow. Anything that we need is wrapped up in the glory. God wants us to change the way we pray. Most prayers are centered on our needs, our issues and our struggles. God does not want His people to beg to be blessed. He wants a people who are hungry for His presence. If we can shift our prayers from asking God for help, to thanking God for His goodness, for life, and for the privilege to come into His presence, then God will manifest Himself and His blessings will be released in our lives.

If we can glorify God, hallow His name, exalt Him, and fall in love with Him alone then God will give us everything that we need and fulfill the desires of our hearts. That's a promise! When we make a conscious decision to shift gears and stop praying for needs and learn how to center our prayers on magnifying the name of the Lord and blessing others, He will bless us beyond measure. Why do people spend time praying for needs? Jesus said,

"Consider the lilies of the field, how they grow; they neither toil or spin... Now if God so clothes the grass of the field, which today is, and tomorrow is thrown into the oven, will He not much more clothe you, O you of little faith" (Matthew 6:28-30) God says, "I don't want to put our people in a need-based situation. I want to strip them to the point where they love only Me. Then all they have to do is desire a thing and it will be given to them."

God does not want us to come to Him only for the sake of receiving things. He is tired of giving cars, houses, money, releasing debts and providing jobs. He wants to do so much more. The purpose of His presence is so much greater. God wants His people to love Him as He loves them. He wants us to worship and honor Him with our whole heart. He wants a pure love relationship with us.

Some church people have reduced the Almighty, Eternal God to paying rent. God does not want you struggling to pay rent. He wants to set you up so that people are paying you rent. Don't go after buildings; go after the God who can provide the buildings. You cannot get close to God without getting blessed. I am sick of religious people. Religious people have the form of godliness, but they lack the demonstration of his power in their lives.

"He brought them forth also with silver and gold: and there was not one feeble person among their tribes." (Psalm 105:37)

When the Israelites came out of Egypt under the cloud of glory, there was no lack in their lives. The Bible says they were delivered from slavery. They were delivered from bondage. They were healed physically. They were blessed financially and their clothes did not wear out for 40 years. Now, that is glory! Every time they needed something to eat, God dropped manna from heaven. The heavens were opened over them and the barrier had been removed. God said it was time to eat and manna fell. Whenever they were thirsty, God cracked a rock open and water was released under the power and by the glory of God.

Now, let me ask you something. Has God changed? While He may not provide manna out of the sky, do you really believe that He would not feed you and provide for your every need? Do you really believe that if you experience His glory you will have to suffer and struggle for your daily sustenance? Do you really think that God would have you worry about your basic needs being met when you are under an open heaven? Not the God I serve!

When God shows up with His glory, the totality of who He is and everything that He possesses comes with it. Glory is coming to some of you individually because God has decided that He can trust you, and He will make sure that you are never in lack. You always will have more than enough because He can trust you to give the balance to somebody else. A word to the wise, "Don't pursue God any longer for the house, the car or finances. Pursue the glory! Increase is in the glory.

My God shall supply all of your needs. How? According to His riches. Where? In glory by Christ Jesus, that He might make known the riches of His glory on the vessels of mercy which He had prepared beforehand for glory. May the eyes of your understanding be enlightened that you may know what is the hope of His calling and what are the riches of the glory of His inheritance in the saints. For this reason, I bow my knees to the Father for whom the whole family in heaven and earth is named, that He would grant you, according to the riches of His glory, to be strengthened with might through the spirit of the inner man the mysteries which have been hidden for ages and for generations but now has been revealed to His saints.

I see something falling. I feel a new birth in the Spirit. I feel this last move before the glory. Here comes the last move. This is what happens when you get on one accord. This is what happens, "not by might, nor by power, but by my Spirit, says the Lord of hosts." He will do it!

CHAPTER 4

Going After The Glory

KINGDOM MANDATE

The Holy Spirit is ushering in a new mandate for the people of God. This is the hour that we must embrace this new mandate that is being poured out and established by God. The first message I preached after recuperating from vocal surgery was, "You Must Be Open For Change." If you are stuck on the old agenda, you risk being left out of this new paradigm shift in the Spirit that will usher in the new mandate of God.

The time is upon us as the people of God to step up and start moving towards their kingdom assignments from heaven. The Holy Spirit wants us to understand that we are not a people

with a generic assignment. We were not sent to the earth realm
to walk around blinded by the darkness of this world. We have
an anointing from God that allows us to deal with current issues
that try to burden our spirits. We are in the earth realm to leave
a deposit of God's glory. So, if you thought you had no purpose
and you were just called to live a passive life, you are wrong.
Your church is waiting; your neighborhood is waiting; your city
is waiting; your state is waiting; your country is waiting for you
to begin manifesting so that the will of God is seen. It is my
heart's cry that everyone who reads this book and who has a
desire burning on the inside of them, will not be left out of this
new mandate for the kingdom.

Are you hungry for Him? Are you hungry for His presence?
Are you hungry for His power? Do you want more of Him?
If you want His glory, start by emptying yourself of anything
that may possibly be a hindrance to the manifestation of His
presence in your life. Go on a sincere spiritual fast, add prayer
and bible study and watch God reveal himself to you. You cannot
orchestrate the manifestation of God's glory. You are not smart
enough. You must simply have a mentality that suggests that
you are hungry for God, that you cannot get enough of Him.
If you are hungry enough, God can make you holy. And if you
are holy, God will show you His glory. Hunger is a prerequisite
for the manifestation of the glory of God.

As a pastor looking out from the pulpit, I see more and more
of God's people walking into the sanctuary worshipping and
praising God regardless of the situations that are trying to bring

them down. When you are walking under the anointing and the mandate of God's glory, no harm can come your way. We are living at a time in history where the prophecies of great men of God from thousands of years ago are being fulfilled with increasing frequency and intensity.

We are living in crucial times. These are not casual times. These are not times to be taken lightly. This generation of which we are a part, is the generation that David said will seek God. Paul warned us that God rewards people who diligently seek him. This is the seeking generation. We want to see God like we have never seen Him before. That's why it is so important for those of us who are leaders in the body of Christ to understand that it is going to be mandatory in this season to stay in step with whatever it is God is doing. Your focus should be, "Lord, whatever you are doing in this season, please do not do it without me." We should not get caught up in the affairs of the world. Rather we should seek to win the world at any cost and the manifestation of His glory will greatly empower us to do that.

Everything that goes on in the church should be designed to glorify God. Even when it is not on the bulletin, God is going to make a demand that will usher in His glory. For this reason, church leaders today must become sensitive to the move and the Spirit of God. You may hear people saying, "That is not how we do it here!" But as the leader, you must follow the voice of God. You must be sensitive to His manifested presence. Don't even look at their faces; just give the mandate that God's glory is here to stay. Let the people know, "If you can't worship with us in the glory, then maybe it is time for you to leave because the glory is staying."

SATURATED WITH THE KNOWLEDGE OF GOD

The Prophet Habakkuk said the whole earth will be filled with the knowledge of the glory of God. No active member in the church will be able to walk around with a lack of knowledge about the glory, as the whole earth will be filled with the knowledge of His glory. My prayer for you is this that you will become saturated with the knowledge of God. Prepare yourself for a great and mighty visitation of the glory of God in the earth. This visitation will impact entire towns, cities, regions and nations. If you receive His glory in this hour, you will not be left out of this awesome demonstration.

This book will wake up everyone who is going to be a part of the outpouring of God's glory in the earth. If you are called to be a part of this incredible dispensation of God's manifested glory then this book will birth something in you to assure you that whatever God is doing in this season, you will not be ignored. The glory is no longer just something for us to talk about or hope for. Not many days from now, a wave of glory will sweep over the body of Christ, and when it does it is going to be huge, it is going to be powerful, and it is going to last for a while.

Once we develop a corporate hunger for the habitation of God's presence and a corporate hunger to experience God's glory, we must then seek to create a comfort zone for the Lord, even if it is a zone of discomfort for man. Believers need to understand that the church does not belong to them. It is simply the selected place of worship that God has assigned for their lives. As Christians, our greatest desire should be to create a comfort zone for the Spirit of the Lord, even if it makes non-believers and some church members nervous or uncomfortable. I desperately want the body of Christ to move away from church as we know it. Our greatest priority in this hour should be to create a comfort zone for the Lord while the greatest priority for the congregation in this season should be going after God's glory.

Every prophet that God has sent to His people throughout the ages has had an encounter, a defining moment or life-changing season in their lives. I am very, very confident that God wants His glory back in the church, beginning with music, worship, prayer and fasting. The time is now for the people of God to begin embracing His glory. Every time we leave church, we should be asking God what just happened because our lives are not the same.

That's why it's going to be important for the church to expose and attack the spirit of religion, which is prevalent throughout the body of Christ. The spirit of religiosity has become the death of revivals everywhere. We have experienced too many revivals where there has been no manifestation of His glory and no outpouring of His Spirit, no healings or breakthroughs. Somehow religion showed up and killed it.

Under this new mandate from God to carry His glory everywhere we go, this religiosity will not be able to ambush future revivals. The mind of Christ has now become available to us. We are wiser and can spot the counterfeit from a distance. In this new dispensation, coming to church will become more than just a ritual or an opportunity to pass the time. The church will once again become the place where we come to have an encounter with the Holy One.

As the body of Christ committed to carrying His glory, we must not only develop a reason for getting hungry for God and His glory but we must also be able to maintain it. We are told in the scriptures, that we go from glory to glory, to glory, which means living in a glorified state at all times. The body of Christ must become dissatisfied with our current level of worship. Some of the light bulbs may be turning on inside your minds and you are realizing that you can no longer tolerate church as it used to be. You have reached your capacity to continue to tolerate the foolishness in the church. Nowadays, the old, off-colored jokes irritate your spirit, and what you laughed at in the past will now cause a frown of disapproval. Places where you used to go to fellowship will now cause you to feel uneasy. Things and situations are not the same. The old you is dying and a new you is emerging one who says, "I want more of God in my life!" You are positioning yourself and doing whatever it takes to get more of Him. Your every move and decisions are taking on new purpose and meaning.

THIRSTY FOR THE GLORY

" O God, You are my God; early will I seek You; my soul thirsts for You; my flesh longs for You in a dry and thirsty land where there is no water. So I have looked for You in the sanctuary, to see Your power and Your glory." (Psalm 63:1-2)

If you are in a dry and thirsty land, I want to encourage you to bring your flesh under subjection and humble yourself and say, "Lord, I need your glory to purify my soul." This kind of honesty will open up your heart to receive God's love for you. The church will become a sanctuary of hope, because sitting at home would no longer be an option or an excuse. It doesn't matter how you get to church; you can walk, run or fly. The Holy Spirit is not interested in the means you use to come, He simply wants you to come and experience the glory. There should be no options as it relates to having a God experience.

As, previously mentioned, the purpose for coming to church is not the choir or the love for the praise and worship. When you leave your home on Sunday morning, you should be thinking, "I don't care what demon is assigned to me today; I am on my way to church to see God's power and glory." Even if everyone else in the church has a different agenda, you will still see His glory, because you have adorned yourself with the right attitude.

When the Bible speaks about equipping the saints in Ephesians, there is no record that ushers, choirs, praise and worship teams or dancers are responsible for equipping the saints of God! They did not make the list. God is not going to hold the ushers accountable for whether or not you see His power and His glory. God knows that there will be some ushers, choirs, praise and worship team members and dancers in many churches with the wrong attitude, who will upset your spirit the minute you walk through the door.

When you wake up in the morning your thoughts should be on the manifested promises of God for your life. The hop and skip in your walk should be from the love of God, not from "I wonder if my hook-up is coming to church today." We are living in a time where play time is over. You cannot allow the lights, the glamour and all the other trappings to twist your focus.

Every parent, guardian and lover of children are expected to teach their children about the glory of God and the importance of reverencing Him in the sanctuary. We should not be seeking the face of God while our children are going to hell. If parents, guardians and lover of children are seeking His glory, so should the child. God wants to reveal Himself to us and to our children every single day, particularly every time we meet to worship Him. God wants to progressively reveal to the children of this generation that He is all they need.

The children of this generation need to know that there is a God who loves them and cares about what's going on in their lives. The world is advancing at warped speed, from television, to the internet. Our children are being bombarded by the attacks of the devil on a daily basis. The only hope is God's saving grace and His glory!

Let me put it like this… the more God moves, the better. The move of God is never stale; it's never stoic; it's never boxed up. Whatever God does is always fresh. He is a God who is always on the move. His mercies are new every morning. The revelation of God and His glory is always progressive. Come seeking His face, seeking His power and seeking His glory.

CONNECTED TO THE SOURCE

God will never do less today than He did yesterday. He enjoys outdoing Himself for our sake. The God we serve is always showing out on our behalf. I have heard this question asked many times, "Will God come through this time and how?" The same glory that showed up on Sunday and Monday is the same glory that shows up on Tuesday and Wednesday, only with a different assignment. Because you are connected to the source even when it looks like all has failed and there is no hope, the glory cloud shows up to remind you that all things are possible with God. He can do anything.

The only question that remains, "Will God be in our midst?" He promised that every time we get together in the name of Jesus, He will be in the midst. As we continue to pursue His glory, the right people and the right relationships will be manifested in our presence. Bring everything that is good and not so good and place it on the altar and walk away. The mandate is heavy and those who are righteous and focused on the glory and the kingdom of God will prevail.

You were born and purposed in the earth for such a time as this, a chosen generation set aside for the use of God. There is a lot riding on the decisions that you make in this hour as it relates to the fulfillment of the kingdom's agenda. There is no such thing as a casual player in the Lord's army. You did not join the army of the Lord of your own free will. There was an unction deep down on the inside of your soul that called you to your rightful position in the kingdom. Before the foundation of the earth, God pre-arranged your every step. You have been chosen as a glory carrier to usher the glory of the Lord back into His church and the lives of His people. What an awesome responsibility the Lord has placed on your shoulders.

As we've shared already, the glory of God comes when the barrier that separates the heavenly realm and the earth realm is removed. When that barrier is removed then God steps out of the heavenly realm into the earth realm and causes people to experience His presence in ways that are witnessed by more than one person. When the glory of God shows up on the scene some will see it, some will hear a sound, and others will smell a sweet aroma. One thing is for certain, when the glory comes, the veil of separation will be torn, removing the barriers that are separating us from His manifested presence.

"Now therefore, I pray, if I have found grace in Your sight, show me now Your way, that I may know You and that I may find grace in Your sight. And consider that this nation is Your people. And

He said, My Presence will go with you, and I will give you rest."
(Exodus 33:13-14)

This scripture must become the cry of every Christian that is seeking a deeper and more meaningful relationship with God. I am not just praying for the churches in the Bahamas; I am also praying for every church that is seeking after the glory of God. The time has come for all of us to stand up and acknowledge that something is missing in the church. Well, that something is His revealed, manifested glory! My prayer is that everyone who wishes to receive this illumination from the Holy Spirit will sensitize their hearts and minds for a fresh visitation from our Lord and Savior. The glory will be restored to the church. This is not something that I am hoping for or wishing to happen; God has made a promise and it is so.

"He who is the Glory of Israel does not lie or change his mind; for he is not a man, that he should change his mind." (1 Samuel 15:29)

I am convinced that there will be some saints who will miss out on the outpouring of this mighty and powerful dispensation of God's glory. I never thought I would see the day when the church would be too blessed to handle blessings and too blessed to reverence God. We have more cars in our driveways than our parents had but we cannot seem to make our way to church. Instead of seeking His presence, the church is seeking His "presents." Has the church sunk so low that it is willing to exchange God for silver and gold? The old saints may not have had as much as we do today, but they seemed happier with less. Maybe they knew something about the manifested glory of God.

The Holy Spirit wants me to ask you a question. Are you prepared for Him to get a little closer? Can God really come into your life and take over? God says, "If you get hungry for me and seek me, I'll get close." I pray that God begins to birth a hunger in your tabernacle that will draw you nearer to Him.

"Who may ascend into the hill of the LORD? Or who may stand in His holy place? He who has clean hands and a pure heart, who has not lifted up his soul to an idol, nor sworn deceitfully. He shall receive blessing from the LORD, and righteousness from the God of his salvation. This is the generation of those who seek Him, who seek Your face. Selah. Lift up your heads, O you gates and be lifted up, you everlasting doors, and the King of glory shall come in." (Psalm 24:3-7)

CHAPTER 5

Living With The Glory

ETERNAL GLORY

I want to live in a world that is filled with the glory of God. I no longer desire to be a Christian with just periodic spasms of the presence of God. I want to live in His presence. I want the glory of God to be commonplace in my life. I don't want to sleep without it. I don't want to be awake without it. I want to live with the glory of God. According to scripture, the glory of the Lord is designed to be eternal in your life.

"But the God of all grace, who hath called us unto his eternal glory by Christ Jesus, after that ye have suffered a while, make you perfect, stablish, strengthen, settle you." (1 Peter 5:10)

The glory of God is not designed to come and go. The glory of God is designed to take you from one level of glory to the next, from glory to glory to glory. The glory of God is eternal. There are many believers who do not want the glory to rest in the House. They simply want a little glory every now and then, because if the glory remains, that means they would have to stop some other activities in their lives. They don't necessarily want permanent glory. They don't want to live in the presence. They just want God to be present and available for whenever they want Him around. They don't want the presence of God to linger. They just want a little touch of His presence and they would be satisfied.

There are some things they have to do that they cannot do with God there. There are some places they have to go where they don't want God to go. When you have traveled as much as I have traveled, and preached as many places as I have preached, and seen as many churches in motion as I have seen, you come to accept certain things. The average believer does not want to experience the manifested presence of God on a consistent basis. They don't want to experience eternal glory. They simply want a taste of temporary glory; a little hit here, and a little fix there but don't hang around because they have some sins to commit and some things to say and do.

Living with the glory means living with His power, His splendor, His magnificence, His wealth, His health, His prosperity and His character. Many people want to live with the glory, but some are convinced that the glory, even though it is eternal, remains with us automatically. No. Once you have the glory, you will not lose it; but if you want to see a demonstration of His glory, you must always take the responsibility for creating an environment for His glory.

Just because you are in a certain place does not mean His glory will be manifested. Just because you are in a church does not mean His glory will be manifested. Remember, there is the omnipresence of God and then the manifested presence of God. You may be carrying the glory, but it may not be manifested because that environment is not conducive for it. I don't expect every church where I preach about the glory to experience the manifested glory because some of them are not creating the environment for the glory to dwell. They want to shout, dance, clap and sing but they don't want the full experience of His glory. They want a little spasm. They want a periodic touchdown, and after they have scored the points, they want to go back to the starting line. They don't want to create an environment in which His glory can dwell. Remember, the real purpose of the church, from God's perspective, is to be the place for His abiding presence. The purpose of the church is not only for us to get together or a place we come just to meet, greet and eat. David said in Psalm 63, we should go to church to see His power and His glory.

THE ENVIRONMENT FOR GLORY

"For the LORD God is a sun and shield: the LORD will give grace and glory: no good thing will he withhold from them that

walk uprightly." (Psalm 84:11)

God is our light and our shield. He is our protection. But He gives grace and glory when the environment is conducive. We should make a great effort to ensure that we create the right atmosphere in which the glory of God can dwell. When we participate in corporate worship we should feed off one another. I grew up going to a little church in the Bahamas, and I did not understand the importance of creating an environment for God's glory. Before church started, every now and then I would hear one of the women of the church shouting, "Glory!" In the middle of the sermon I heard, "Glory!" My friends and I would laugh and say that the women were crazy but what they were doing was feeding off one another. They were creating an environment conducive for His glory. They wanted the manifested presence of God to be seen in that service.

The 21st century church does not create an environment for His glory. The 21st century church creates an environment for fellowship; we rarely create an environment for glory. God never calls a people to have glory; He calls a people to carry glory. The body of Christ must learn how to feed off each other.

Ushers in the Lord's church believe that their only responsibility to God is to usher. Musicians believe that their only responsibility to God is to play. It doesn't matter how they live their lives, as long as they are performing their functions, they think they are in order. The choir's responsibility, as far as they are concerned, is to just sing at their appointed time. If the people in the pew do not feel like they are worshipping God, they instantly categorize the choir as 'entertaining'. Believers must learn how to get one accord but in order to do that we have to create and maintain an environment for the glory to inhabit.

For example, if I wanted to create an environment for healing, I would find someone who is not well. Now, I don't have to be sick to feed off of them. I would just cry out, "Oh God, deliver me!" Then I would cry out, "Oh God, deliver us!" I may not be sick, but we are one. If one needs healing, we all need healing.

The body of Christ is too fragmented, that is why so many people are still in bondage. When they come to the church for deliverance in a particular area, the church sometimes isolates them. Here's what we do. We get caught up and brag about the fact that we are praising God for our house; we just don't have it yet. "I'm thanking God for my breakthrough; I just don't have it yet;" "I'm giving God praise for my promotion. I know God will make a way. I just don't have it yet." But we never say, "I'm praising God for healing me of AIDS, I just don't see the physical manifestation of my healing." No, we don't say anything like that. We say that the house is coming, the car is coming, the promotion is coming, money is coming but we don't say anything about the healing from sicknesses coming. You can stop sickness in its track before it gets to you, but in order to do that, we have to be able to create an environment for His glory. Sickness, disease, lack and shortage are all eradicated in an environment that has been prepared to house His glory.

"For the LORD God is a sun and shield: the LORD will give grace and glory: no good thing will he withhold from them that walk uprightly." (Psalm 84:11)

When God creates an environment for glory, He does not keep anything good from you. Promotions are good, marriage is good, increase is good, the spirit of joy is good, and the spirit of peace is good. God does not keep any good thing away from you when an environment of glory is created. When you live with the glory and you are cognizant of His manifested presence in your midst, whatever God keeps away from you is kept away from you for a reason; it is either not good for you or it is not good for you at that particular time. God may not be keeping it away from you; He may be keeping it for you because if He gives it to you at that particular time it may damage you.

What we need more than anything else is an environment of glory created where we have the opportunity and the privilege to live with the glory 24 hours a day, seven days a week.

THE LANGUAGE OF HEAVEN

"In the year that king Uzziah died I saw also the LORD sitting upon a throne, high and lifted up, and his train filled the temple. Above it stood the seraphims: each one had six wings; with twain he covered his face, and with twain he covered his feet, and with twain he did fly. And one cried unto another, and said, Holy, holy, holy, is the LORD of hosts: the whole earth is full of his glory." (Isaiah 6:1-3)

I am a citizen of The Bahamas and English is the official language of The Bahamas but in my estimation it is not really 'the language' of the Bahamas. The language of the Bahamas is a Bahamian dialect (a derivative of the English language). English is the language of the Queen of England. Language matters because if you do not speak the language of a people you will not be able to communicate effectively whenever you are in their company. Likewise, when we come into the presence of God, if we are not speaking the language of heaven, we will not be able to effectively communicate with him.

What is the language of heaven? The language of heaven is, "Holy, Holy, Holy." When the language of heaven is spoken among a people, the place is filled with the glory of the Lord. In Isaiah 6:1, the scripture says that the seraphim cried out to one another, "Holy, Holy, Holy." They fed each other. They did not cry out to God. One cried to another.

When one group cried out "Holy," another group cried out "Holy," and so on and so on. It was a continual effect of worship, until the whole earth was filled with the glory of the God. Notice, the angels were not crying out to God calling Him holy. God is fully aware that He is holy. They were reminding each other that God is holy.

You cannot say the whole earth is full of His glory unless you are experiencing glory right here and right now. Most people do not speak the language of heaven because they do not want to live the language of heaven. If we start crying out "Holy," that will remind us of who God is and remind us of who we are. *"Because it is written, Be ye holy; for I am holy."* (1 Peter 1:16) Every time you utter the word "Holy," it reminds you of what you should be. Many people do not want to be reminded of their true identify in God. Therefore, they choose not to speak the language.

The apostles, pastors, teachers, evangelists and prophets should be reminding the people of their true identity. We should be setting a standard for living that challenges and encourages the body of Christ to walk in the true identify of who they are – HOLY! Many church leaders are not insisting that their members live right. They are not requiring that their people uphold a standard of living that emanates the revealed, manifested presence of God.

Some leaders may not require their members to live a life of holiness, because they don't want to live holy. If I tell you to be holy, then that forces me to live holy. You rarely hear sermons preached on holiness from the pulpit. You rarely hear sermons preached on righteousness. If you want to be a popular preacher in this 21st century, you have to preach blessings or miracles. You have to be able to tell people to turn around three times and watch God move. But without holiness, none of us can see God. That is the language of heaven. (Hebrews 12:14)

If you want to maintain an environment for God's glory to dwell in the church, you must speak the language of heaven often. "Holy, Holy, Holy" brings glory. "Holy, Holy, Holy" keeps the glory of God resting in the house. Take away the "Holy, Holy, Holy" and there goes the glory.

"And the posts of the door moved at the voice of him that cried, and the house was filled with smoke. Then said I, Woe is me! for I am undone; because I am a man of unclean lips, and I dwell in the midst of a people of unclean lips: for mine eyes have seen the King, the LORD of hosts." (Isaiah 6:4-5)

In Isaiah 6, we see the angels were crying out to each other and because there was such a holy cry in the house, the posts of the door were shaken. I am ready to be a part of a church that experiences His glory from the moment you walk into the sanctuary. One where the environment is so glory focused that the people are crying, "Holy, Holy, Holy" to the extent that you can feel the building moving. That is power!

When the house is filled with the glory of God, people cannot stay in their sins. Most church people do not want the glory of God to rest in the church, because they will either have to leave the church or it will force them to repent. When the glory fills the house, if the bishop, the pastor or the preacher has un-confessed sins, he will find himself at the altar confessing his sins. Many people are afraid to experience the glory because they are comfortable with their sin. I have been through so much in my life that I am sold out for the things of God. I understand that if I am going to carry the glory of God, my body has to be the temple of the living God.

Go to the modern-day church anywhere around the world and you will not hear people crying out, "Holy, Holy, Holy is the Lord God of Hosts." Instead, you will hear, "Bless me, Jesus. Do it for me one more time, Lord or I need a miracle Jesus." You won't hear people coming in saying, "Lord, I love you." You will hear people saying, "Oh God, you promised to supply all my needs according to your riches in Glory by Christ Jesus." They want the riches of God but they don't want the glory of God because His glory requires something from them.

When you have been imbued with an anointing that touches the globe, it is your responsibility to be able to create an environment conducive for God's glory to dwell at all times. This is not a temporary assignment. It is supposed to be permanent, going from glory to glory to glory. When the choir sings, it should be their intent to create an environment for His glory. The intent should not be to produce "stars." The focus should be on creating a worship experience that assists in creating an environment for God's glory.

Some people come to church and serve just to escape their circumstances. Their response is usually, "Do you know the hell I went through this week? I came here looking for a breakthrough, not to create anything. I came to get something. I could not wait to get to church because I knew God was going to meet me here." Do you think God will meet where His manifested presence is dwelling just because you want a breakthrough? If you want a breakthrough, create the environment but make sure that is not your focus. You should focused on "creating."

If you create, you will see manifestation. But you will not see if you do not create!

CREATING AN ENVIRONMENT FOR GLORY

We have to know how to create an environment of glory that causes the hypocrites to become wretched. We know that there will always be hypocrites in the church; that will not stop until Jesus comes. But at least let's make them wretched, so they will make a turn. When people tell me, "I'm not coming to church because there are too many hypocrites there," I say to them, "Oh, there is room for one more."

So many believers are so busy trying "to do" that they never have time "to be;" and as a result, we never "become." "I have to do this, and I have to do that." "We have to hurry up because we are on duty." "I have to serve today." Some of your most dedicated workers in the church are among the weakest believers because they never get to grow. They are too busy.

Many churches build an environment for commitment, which is often demonstrated by carrying out tasks and completing assignments. "Don't worry about God; just be committed to your church. Don't worry about holiness; just be committed to your pastor." People are trained to be loyal to their church more so than to God. "Don't worry about all of this God stuff. Do what you are assigned to do. After all, God will judge you by how you perform." That's what we tell our people. We don't tell them to be holy as God is holy.

I expect our armor bearers to commit more than their time to the service of the ministry. I expect those who work in my office to represent more than their job assignments. If they are committed? to the work of the kingdom, prayer, praise and worship, there should be an atmosphere that suggests an environment of glory around them.

CHAPTER 6

Creating An Environment For The Glory

ENVIRONMENT CREATORS

The average believer wants God to show up so that they can know that He is real, but they are not ready for all that is required for eternal glory. I am trying to get the members of Mount Tabor to be appreciative of the eternal weight of glory. That does not mean that every service will be the same but it means that they will be living with the Glory, with its power, splendor, magnificence, wealth, health, prosperity, character and everything that He is.

Many Christians want to live with the glory, but some are convinced that the glory remains with us automatically. No. Once you have the Glory, you will not lose it but if you want to see a demonstration of it, you must take the responsibility for creating an environment for the glory. Don't think that because you are certain places that the Glory will be manifested. Don't mix up God's omnipresence with His manifested presence. You may be carrying the glory, but it may not be manifested because the environment may not be conducive for it.

Every church should have a few people designated as "environment creators," so that every time we show up the Glory of God will be manifested. I am so tired of people coming into God's House with an air of importance and acting as if it is all about them. When I go to church, I don't go to see anybody but God. Our first and most important announcement for the week should be, "The King is here!" We should be excited that we have come to worship the King. As a Pastor, one of the greatest announcements that I can make in a worship service is to say, "The King Is Here!"

Recently, our church was going though a consecration period. During that period, after prayerful consideration, I shifted the services around saturating the people with prayers and songs of worship. One Sunday morning, the Holy Spirit interrupted the 'flow'. After the second prayer God commanded me to preach. Do you think I paused to look around to see how the other people who were supposed to pray felt or to see how the choir felt because they did not sing or to see how the praise and worship team felt because they did not sing? No! I did not have time to think about flesh. When the King showed up everything else was off the agenda.

It is amazing to me how the body of Christ gets more excited about what God does, than who God is. It is amazing that in the 21st century, the body of Christ finds it easier to celebrate a blessing from God than to celebrate God for being God. If someone at the church is blessed with a car, the people will celebrate. They will run, shout and dance. In this season, we must be sensitized to the fact that not everyone will be excited about being a carrier of God's glory. Make no mistake, blessings come with the glory but so does sacrifice. Can you imagine being a part of a church where at the sound of the name of JESUS people still get excited not because of what He did but at the sound of His name?

If God is our source, every time we get a chance to praise Him we should do it. If God is truly our source, we do not have to wait for supply to have a real celebration. All we have to do is remember who the source is.

REMOVING BARRIERS

"For the LORD God is a sun and shield: the LORD will give grace and glory: no good thing will he withhold from them that walk uprightly." (Psalm 84:11)

God is our light and our protection. He is our sun and our shield. He gives grace and glory but only when the environment is conducive. In an earlier chapter, I emphasized that glory comes when there is a collision between the heavenly realm and the earthly realm, when the barrier that separates the two realms is removed.

Be aware that the devil will use the spirit of division to create barriers within the body of Christ. *"Now the works of the flesh are evident, which are: adultery,[a] fornication, uncleanness, lewdness, [20] idolatry, sorcery, hatred, contentions, jealousies, outbursts of wrath, selfish ambitions, dissensions, heresies, [21] envy, murders,[b] drunkenness, revelries, and the like; of which I tell you beforehand, just as I also told you in time past, that those who practice such things will not inherit the kingdom of God."* (Galatians 5:19-21)

Let me tell you how you can remove barriers. You must create an environment of glory. Nothing and no one can withstand the revealed, manifested power and presence of Almighty God. When the wave of glory comes, change will come, restoration will come, and renewal come.

CHAPTER 7

Revival Fires

"Even the mystery which hath been hid from ages and from generations, but now is made manifest to his saints: To whom God would make known what is the riches of the glory of this mystery among the Gentiles; which is Christ in you, the hope of glory." (Colossians 1: 26-27)

The heart of God is to draw near to His people. If we draw near to God, He will draw near to us. While the heart of God is to draw near to His people, He certainly wants us to make the first move. He wants us to gravitate towards Him so that He can draw near to us. I hear God saying, "Come, My child; all things are now ready, but I am waiting for you to make the very first move."

He wants people to go to any church that bears His Name and where they can find His presence. It would be awesome if in every church people could walk in and discover that the presence of the Lord is there! That would be wonderful. In many churches, however, we can see that the pulpit and the pews are there, we can see them everywhere, but no presence.

OUR FIRST LOVE

As we have been discussing throughout this book, the real purpose of the church, from God's perspective, is for the church to be the place for God's abiding presence. The heart of God is to draw near to His people. From the inception of the church, God's desire has always been for the church to be a reflection of the beauty, the majesty, and the power of Jesus by filling the church with Himself, His power, and His glory. God never intended for His church to abandon the reality of His presence. He never intended for His people to leave their first love, which is being in His presence.

God never intended for His church to become dead, stale and boring. Revival is actually God's second choice. God's desire is that He would not have to revive His church because His original intention was for the church to never leave her first love. He never intended for the church to become dead enough, stale enough, and boring enough that it would need a revival. Given the realities of our times and the stubbornness of His people, revival became a necessary second choice.

People who you see in church frequently · are still there

because they have not lost their first love. They may be slipping and sliding, shoving and jiving but there is still something in them that makes them want to come into the house of the Lord. Those are not the ones we should be concerned about. There are thousands outside of the church who never come around and never make a contribution to the work of God for the kingdom. They are the ones we must go after. We must stop beating up those in the House who have become and are still wounded; at least they are still in a position to be healed, to grow and to experience the glory.

If you live long enough you will find that sooner or later you will fall short of the glory of God; and when you do, you want to make sure that there is somebody who is spiritual around who will aid you in your restoration and bring you back into proper alignment with the word of God and the kingdom of God. I am not quick to condemn people. I do not push people down, especially when I see them falling. I believe that it is the responsibility of the spiritually minded to take them by the hand and pull them up and say, "I know what you are dealing with. I know what you are going through. But if you hold my hand, I will walk you through this."

God has this habit of not letting us all fall at the same time. Isn't He a good God? That is why He said the strong should bear up the weak. We should want to lift up the fallen and rescue the perishing. If you are strong today, it is not because you are 'all that'; it is because God fixed you so you can have the strength to pull up someone who is weak today.

"For My people have committed two evils: They have forsaken Me, the fountain of living waters, and hewn themselves cisterns— broken cisterns that can hold no water. (Jeremiah 13:2)

Jeremiah had to rebuke Israel because they had forsaken God's presence for other things. They preferred to replace God, the fountain of living water, for cisterns that could hold no water. The Israelites, God's chosen people, had committed two sins. Number one, they had forsaken God; and number two, they had built for themselves broken cisterns that could hold no water.

In the Old Testament, we find a pattern of God appearing unto His people. In the New Testament, his appearances were primarily based on the experiences of His disciples. In the early days of the New Testament church, there were no bibles or Christian television. However, what they did have were testimonies that were based upon their own experiences with God. The thing that perplexed the early church was not correct doctrine and theology or church systems, programs and plans. What perplexed the early church was the fact that their leaders were ordinary people who had amazing encounters with God. They were people who were willing to come under an open heaven and allow God to touch them and change them, people who had a taste of glory, and were not imprisoned by religious doctrine and bogged down in systems. They were not focused on their denominations or what to wear and what not to wear and how they looked. The early church was built by ordinary people who had been touched by God and changed by His glory not on legalism.

THE WORLD IS WAITING

"For I consider that the sufferings of this present time are not worthy to be compared with the glory which shall be revealed in us. For the earnest expectation of the creation eagerly waits for the revealing of the sons of God." (Romans 8:18-19)

Whenever the glory of the Lord in heaven is revealed, there will be reaction to it. The world is dying to see the revelation of God's power, God's life, God's love and God's glory in us. We say we are Christians, but the world is tired of only seeing us. The world wants to see the God in us. The world wants to see the power of God working through us. The world wants to see our faith in action in our own individual lives. The world wants to see the church of the living God filled with Him instead of us.

All over the world, there are Christian believers who try to exalt themselves higher than the Lord. They want to take over. As a result, so many preachers and church leaders are afraid of the glory of God because once God comes with His glory, He has to be in charge. Even this wicked world has a longing to see God in us. Therefore, our responsibility as believers is submit to God and stop talking about being a Christian.

Our religious doctrines and practices are not what they eagerly await. They want and need to see the power of God working in us and through us. They want to know and need to know that the God that we are preaching about is admired and adored by us. They want to see that the God that we are preaching about has no problem showing Himself strong in us. Many Christians have become the laughing stock of unbelievers when we preach about the power of God and there is no evidence of what we proclaim in our lives.

This is very often the case because the church is filled with people who have walked away from their first love. Sometimes we fall short of the glory of God and sometimes we are mean, disobedient and stiff-necked as it relates to the things of God. That is why ever so often, the church needs reviving. We need revival fire.

Revival is a byproduct of the manifestation of the glory of God. It is difficult for people to be touched with the glory of God without the manifestation of revival. Again, the glory of God comes when there is a collision between the heavenly realm and the earth realm. The glory of God comes when the barrier that separates the two realms is removed and God in all of His splendor, steps out of the realm of heaven into the earth realm and touches people in a way where they can experience God with one of their five senses.

HISTORIC REVIVALS

Let's look at some of the great revivals of the past.

JOHN WESLEY: THE FOUNDER OF METHODISM

John Wesley was probably the most well known revivalist.

Born in 1703, John Wesley was the founder of Methodism. In 1737, he became an Anglican priest, very stiff and cold in his presentation of the Word. John Wesley experienced a touch of the glory of God. However, the Anglican Church was not ready for the type of spiritual movement that John Wesley presented, and as a result, he left the Anglican church and formed the Methodist movement.

After he formed the Methodist movement, Wesley became a carrier of God's glory. While he was preaching and bringing forth the word of God, people would fall under the anointing, even without him laying his hands on them. Wesley was a starchy, cold, stiff, Anglican priest, who experienced God and received a touch of God's glory. Instead of the Anglican church receiving him, they pushed him away thereby giving way to the formation of the Methodist movement. One touch of God's glory turned his life around and put him in line with his divine assignment. God used him to touch the lives of millions of people and to bring about a dramatic change around the world. Many of the hymns we sing today were written by John Wesley or his brother, Charles.

In January, 1739, the Methodist/Pentecost movement erupted. It is said that this movement was one of the most powerful moves the world has seen since the day of Pentecost. Thousands came from around the world to be in the meetings and to experience God's power and glory.

GEORGE WHITFIELD

George Whitfield, one of John Wesley's workers, who was a part of his team when this Methodist/Pentecost movement erupted, experienced the glory of God in such a powerful way that when he started to preach and minister at the meetings in England, he would pack the house. It is reported that in one of the services, he saw more than 10,000 people slain under the power of the Holy Ghost. (Note: that was not the number of people in attendance; that was the number of people who were slain in the Spirit.)

People would climb into trees in order to get close enough to hear him preach. At one point, he had to put ushers around the trees to stop people from climbing the trees because he noticed that people were being slain in the Spirit and falling out of the trees. The record shows that wherever Whitfield went, the power and the glory of God followed him.

JONATHAN EDWARDS

Jonathan Edwards was born in 1703. Some people regard him as the greatest American theologian who ever lived. Others have described him as having the greatest mind that America has produced. God used this sharp scholar to birth revival in America. On July 8, 1741, Edwards preached a sermon in Connecticut entitled, "Sinners in the Hands of an Angry God." In the middle of his preaching, it is recorded that the heavens opened over Connecticut and the glory of God fell on the city. That sermon sparked the beginning of what became known as the "Great Awakening" in America

In 1741, the presence of God was so heavy that the people were overcome with the power and the glory of God during revival meetings. Many of them never made it home in the evenings. They stayed where they were slain in the Holy Ghost, motionless under the power of God throughout the night.

CHARLES FINNEY

In the 1800's, a man by the name of Charles Finney came on the scene. He was known as one of the greatest revivalists in American history. Because of the level of the glory of God that he carried, entire cities were saved by the power of God. Charles Finney was a praying man. From 1857 to 1859, there was a great revival in America known as the Prayer Revival. In a two-year period, more than 10% of the 30 million people living in America at that time were saved, that is more than 300,000 people. When Finney held revivals in New England, over 200 towns and cities would stop everything at twelve noon in order to have noonday prayer meetings.

When he held revival meetings in Washington, D.C., courtrooms were shutting down at twelve noon and workers would gather on the lawn of the U.S. Capitol to pray for America. Studies show that 25 years later, 75% of all of the people who were saved during Finney's revivals were still serving God and the reports of back-sliding were very low.

Today, people are receiving, what I call, "popcorn salvation," saved today, back-sliding tomorrow. But in centuries past when the people experienced the glory of the Lord, they were committed to serving Him and stayed saved. Twenty-five years later, you could still find them serving God.

THE GREAT WELSH REVIVAL

The 20th century was impacted by revivals around the world. The first and probably the largest revival to erupt in the 20th century was the Great Welsh Revival. God used one man, by the name of Evan Roberts, and 17 teenagers to birth this revival. They made up their minds that they were going to gather to pray and were not coming out of the church until the power of God fell. (As parents, we are to train our children in the ways of the Lord. I get concerned when I see the roles reversed and teenagers controlling parents.)

One night when they were locked in the church in prayer, the windows of heaven began to open and the glory of the Lord covered Wales in such a great way that the Great Welsh Revival was sparked. Someone described it as an unseen river that came over entire towns.

There were towns and cities in Wales that had to lay off entire police force for three years because there was nothing for them to do. There was no crime. There were towns that had to close the courthouses because there were no cases to try. One man and 17 teenagers ushered in a revival that caused every bar in Wales to close its doors, gambling houses to shut down, and the record is that prostitution went out of business.

I believe that this is the answer for the escalating crime rate all over the world. It is not going to be by might, nor by power; but I believe it is going to be by a people crying out in the Spirit and saying, "Lord, send us your glory."

THE HEBRIDES REVIVAL

In 1949, a great example of the glory of God descending upon a geographical area was experienced. Between 1948 and 1951, the people of the Hebrides Islands, a series of islands off the west coast of Scotland, experienced what was called the Hebrides Revival. According to the records, revival erupted in the Hebrides Islands, but the entire region was saturated with the glory of God. The glory was so intense that visitors coming into the area were impacted. As a result, a major harvest of souls was ushered into the kingdom.

During the Hebrides Revival, 75% of the country's population was saved, of which most of the people had never been to church. The glory of God was so strong it was over the whole island. Wherever there were people, God was saving them.

THE AZUSA STREET REVIVAL (1996)

Most believers are familiar with the Azusa Street Revival, the largest Pentecostal revival that ever hit the United States. On Father's Day 1996, revival erupted in Pensacola, Florida, where thousands of people were touched and saved because of the direct confrontation with God.

A WAVE OF GLORY

In November 2002, we were in the middle of our "Week In The Word Conference". A woman of God stepped into the pulpit that was led by a man who only 10 years before was preaching against female preachers. Prophetess Juanita Bynum stepped into the pulpit at Mount Tabor and never read a scripture. From the time she got up God took a hold of her. The Prime Minister of The Bahamas as well as the president of the Senate and four members of the cabinet were present. She was led by God to ask all of the men who were not afraid to take off their jackets, loosen their ties, and roll up their shirt sleeves. She then challenged us to go into our downtown area for a gathering and declare that revival was coming to the Bahamas.

The next day, Prophetess Bynum came to the midday session of the conference and in the middle of her sermon, I interrupted her and shared that "God wants us to do something together fast." At that moment, "Revival is Here," was birthed. In February 2003, "Revival Is Here" started and more than 40,000 people filled the open field at Clifford Park, (the National Park in Nassau, Bahamas) each night. People came from as far north as Iceland and as far south as Australia. Services were held at 7:00 in the evening, 11:00 at night,1:00 in the morning and again at 5:00 a.m. for an early morning service. Some people would take their lunch breaks so that they could attend the midday service at Mount Tabor and would be back on the park for 7:00 in the evening. Every service was filled to capacity and God moved mightily in them all. Revival was in the land.

On the closing night of the revival, the Prime Minister of The Bahamas at that time, The Rt. Honorable Perry Gladstone Christie, addressed the nation and asked me to extend the revival for one more day. That Friday we had a midday service in the park for children. The leaders of the school system gave us trouble and did not cooperate with closing the schools for that day, but the children were so filled with the glory of God that they didn't go to school. More than 60,000 young people showed up at Clifford Park, and over 2,000 were saved. Revival was in the land.

On the following Monday, at the end of revival, the police commissioner made a public statement. He said that we needed to have another revival because from Monday to Friday of the revival, there were no crimes reported throughout the country. Let me reiterate, I have discovered the answer to the high crime rate and violence in our nations… "Lord, send us your glory!"

"And it shall come to pass afterward, that I will pour out my spirit upon all flesh; and your sons and your daughters shall prophesy, your old men shall dream dreams, your young men shall see visions: And also upon the servants and upon the handmaids in those days will I pour out my spirit." (Joel 2:28-29)

We need a shake-up in the church, starting with parents. I believe that when revival comes we will not hear about violence in the schools as often. The principals will be calling churches asking them if they have any counselors that can come to the schools because revival has broken out on the school campuses. Do not wait until some young person breaks into your house to pray for revival. Do not wait until murder, rape or some other violent crime comes to your door. Now is the time for us to cry out, "Lord, show us your glory!"

Since the beginning of the new millennium, the glory of God has been falling all over the world. In the very near future, I believe we are going to see a wave of God's glory touching nations. Revival comes to a nation when there is a revelation of God's manifested, glorified presence touching the lives of people in a real and powerful way. Revival is the work of the Holy Spirit. Man cannot start revival but man can stop it by refusing to yield to what God is doing.

The Hebrides Revival that changed the whole country of Wales, to the point where they had to lay off police officers, close barrooms, courthouses, and whorehouses was started by a man in the 1700's, and God's manifested glory has been lingering throughout the earth ever since, seeking to save and rescue others. I believe that no one who really wants a change in their life will be left out. If you are having challenges at home, school or on the job, if you are struggling in relationships with friends, family or parents, if you are having challenges with some of your children, do not be discouraged. The devil got a glimpse of the plans that God has for you and he is trying to ruin them before God can manifest His power through you. God wants you and your children to operate in His full, manifested presence and to walk according to His course of destiny for your life.

Speak words of life over your children: "The devil will not have you! God has His hands on you and you will manifest His power, authority and glory!" I have no doubt that many children, by the power of God, will be filled with the Holy Spirit. God will use some of your children to carry the revival fire around the world. Some will become catalysts for the youth revival that is about to hit nations. God will never do less today than He did yesterday.

The revelation of God is always progressive. Do not simply expect God to repeat what you saw Him do in the days of the Bible. Do not expect to simply see a repeat of what He did in the 1700's, 1800's and 1900's. In this dispensation, God will exceed what He has already done among men. Expect greater works!

WHY WILL GOD MOVE LIKE THIS?

- So that the glory will be revealed (John 11:4)
- So that people will believe in Him (John 14:11)
- So that He may destroy the works of the devil (1 John 3:8)

It won't be long now before the body of Christ rises up in the nations like a mighty army. That is a prophecy. God is reviving His church again. Not too long from now, the church is going to take its rightful place in the nations around the world and act as the voice of God. When God speaks, something has to happen. There will be a shaking real soon as a result of the glory of God that is going to come. God is raising up a people and building such an understanding of His Glory because He does not want to see a revival of the church aborted.

We are entering an appointed time on God's agenda. We are getting ready to witness a season in which God will open up the heavens and reveal Himself in the earth by the demonstration of His power and His glory. Whenever the heavenly realm overlaps into the earth realm, all limitations are removed and anything becomes possible.

- When the glory of God comes, expect a turnaround in your personal situation.
- When the glory of God comes, you will see God stepping into the arena of your life and turning the tide in your favor. Every valley shall be exalted, every mountain made low, the crooked paths shall be made straight and the rough places smooth.

It is impossible to separate the glory of God from the power of God, the wisdom of God, the love of God and the provision of God. Blessings and breakthrough become easy in an environment of glory, which creates an atmosphere for miracles.

CHAPTER 8

Using Your Mouth

"And some of them said, Could not this man, which opened the eyes of the blind, have caused that even this man should not have died? Jesus therefore again groaning in himself cometh to the grave. It was a cave, and a stone lay upon it. Jesus said, Take ye away the stone. Martha, the sister of him that was dead, saith unto him, Lord, by this time he stinkett: for he hath been dead four days. Jesus saith unto her, Said I not unto thee, that, if thou wouldest bleive, thou shouldest see the glory of God?" (John 11:37-40)

CARRY THE GLORY

Glory is mentioned 510 times in the Bible, and 393 of those times it was mentioned as something being given to God. The time has come for the parading of flesh to vanish from the

House of God. Our fleshly thoughts, actions and motives must come under the surrender of the Holy Spirit. We can't spend the rest of our lives pursuing His glory. We must position ourselves to experience the glory and then to become glory carriers. In order to do this, we must start by putting a demand on our flesh to submit to God and His glory. This is the time for us to let God be totally God. We have to pursue His glory.

We have power over the flesh by speaking the word of God. Proverbs 18:21 says, *"Death and life [are] in the power of the tongue: and they that love it shall eat the fruit thereof."* Therefore, the glory of God must become an active part of our daily living. Pursuing the glory means you are trying to capture the glory in your life, but living with the glory means you are living in an environment that is conducive for the miraculous; and wherever there is an environment conducive for the miraculous, you can always expect the supernatural.

We do not need to have God in our midst to have church because so many of us know how to do that professionally. We could come to a worship service for three hours, have church and God is no where in the house. Everywhere I go I meet people who say they are sick and tired of church as we know it to exist today. There are people who are ready for real, authentic worship and praise encounters with God. Many know how to do church well. But now God is in search of a people who will worship Him in spirit and in truth and in the very beauty of holiness.

Holiness is not a denomination. Holiness is beautiful. Holiness is a mindset that says, "I am sold out to God." Holiness is not a dress code. It is a decision that in Him I live, and move and have my being. Holiness is not an elimination of makeup. Holiness is a choice, that my body is the temple of the Lord. We need God and His glory if we are to achieve a lifestyle of holiness. We need His presence in the church for the glory to fall. But if God does not show up, there is no glory; and if there is no glory, we will be stuck like millions of other saints in churches around the world, "having a form of godliness but denying its power." (2 Timothy 3:5) There are enough religious programs on television to stay at home and have church, if that's all you want.

The Holy Spirit is going to show up at our churches and drop His glory without our permission. Guess what? There is nothing the pastor, the prophet or the apostle can do to hinder this visitation from God. The whole earth shall be filled with His glory. Many of our sanctuaries are going to experience His glory and manifested promises. God is getting ready to fill His house with His glory. What is equally important, however, is that we as believers do not simply experience corporate glory. We must do all that we can to ensure that God's glory also rests upon our lives. The following passages of scripture help us understand how to connect with God's glory.

OH, THE GLORY!

"And behold, an angel of the Lord stood before them, and the glory of the Lord shone around them, and they were greatly afraid.

Then the angel said to them, "Do not be afraid, for behold, I bring you good tidings of great joy which will be to all people." (Luke 2:9-10)

The angels created glory for the announcement of the birth of Christ. Now, understand what was happening. The angels created an atmosphere of glory in order to announce the birth of the Christ child, which means the angels were now letting the shepherds know that what is in heaven is about to come to the earth. In other words, they were making the announcement that the barrier that separates the two realms is about to be removed.

The glory will always frighten you because glory takes you out of your comfort zone. When the glory comes, it is all God. You are no longer in charge. Glory never brings bad tidings. Glory is always accompanied with joy. The Hebrew word for "glory" is KABOD, which means, "a thought, a hunch, a hint, a sense of," which is made manifest with the mouth.

In an atmosphere where the glory is present, God will often give you a thought, a hunch, a hint and a sense that it is your set time for something to be released into the atmosphere and into the earthly realm. Once you open your mouth and start releasing praise and adoration into the atmosphere, you immediately begin to shift things around. You are never left in the dark when you live with God's glory. You become positioned to experience life as it is in heaven, let it be in the earth. Whatever God's will is in heaven, I want you to begin experiencing it on the earth and living in the hopes to accomplish that.

SAY SOMETHING

"Then I looked, and I heard the voice of many angels around the throne, the living creatures, and the elders; and the number of them was ten thousand times ten thousand, and thousands of thousands, saying with a loud voice: Worthy is the Lamb who was slain to receive power and riches and wisdom, and strength and honor and glory and blessing!" (Revelation 5:11-12)

The church can no longer stay silent and expect to receive the blessings of God. Christians must step outside of their comfort zone and begin to speak with a loud voice, "Worthy is the Lamb of God." The fact of the matter is when you live with the glory, you cannot escape the blessings of God.

Riches, wisdom, strength and glory are yours in this season. You have not because you refuse to open your mouth and proclaim God's greatness in the land. You have no one to blame for this but yourself. It's not the devil's doing, nor is God holding something back from you. If you don't start opening your mouth and acknowledging His greatness, the glory of God will pass you by.

"And every creature which is in heaven and on the earth and under the earth and such as are in the sea, and all that are in them, I heard saying: Blessing and honor and glory and power [Be] to Him who sits on the throne, And to the Lamb, forever and ever!" (Revelation 5:13)

We had our beginning with God in heaven, and by His love and grace we were sent to the earth to complete our mission.

When you look at the above scripture, it lets us know that everything that was created must be heard saying, "Blessing and honor and glory and power [Be] to Him who sits on the throne, and to the Lamb, forever and ever!"

There is no excuse for not praising God with your mouth. There is a tone that you set in your environment that brings tranquility when you start having God-like conversations. What once looked impossible becomes granted to you because of the favor of God on your life. This is the direct result of you giving God His honor and due respect. I know you may be thinking, "Does it really take all of that?" My response is, Yes, it does!

"After these things I heard a loud voice of a great multitude in heaven, saying, Alleluia! Salvation and glory and honor and power belong to the Lord our God!" (Revelation 19:1)

Did you notice the exclamation point after Alleluia? The writer is trying to get your attention. Right now, stop what you're doing and say "Alleluia!" and put an exclamation point mark after it. This may sound pointless, but it is it important. An exclamation point is like riding down the road at top speed and the traffic light turns red. You are now forced to come to an immediate stop. The exclamation point after "Alleluia" forces us to stop for a moment and give God praise. After recognizing God for being God, we can continue saying, "Salvation and glory and power belong to you, Lord."

DON'T MISHANDLE THE GLORY

"Give unto the LORD the glory due to His name; Worship the LORD in the beauty of holiness. The voice of the LORD [is] over the waters; The God of glory thunders; The LORD [is] over many waters." (Psalm 29:2-3)

You cannot act feeble minded while you are in the process of giving God glory. You cannot play around when you are handling His glory. You cannot even pretend to act weary or tired when you are dealing with God's glory. The glory of God is not a light weight. It takes tremendous spiritual strength to carry it. *"For the earth will be filled with the knowledge of the glory of the LORD, as the waters cover the sea."* (Habakkuk 2:14)

When we come into an environment where the glory is manifested, the voice of God will be heard; and at that point you will begin to see things happen. Incidentally, when life starts getting a little crazy, 'take a time out' and shout "Glory to the King!" Again, it is important to understand that in order to live with the glory you must begin using your mouth.

"Then those who feared the LORD spoke to one another, And the LORD listened and heard [them]; So a book of remembrance was written before Him For those who fear the LORD And who meditate on His name." (Malachi 3:16)

"Then those who feared the Lord spoke to one another…" The word "feared" translated means "worship." While worshipping before God you cannot ignore your brother and sister who are in your midst. If God is the only one you want to talk to, you need to step out of the presence of God and start praying because in worship we are required to speak to one another.

The Book of Remembrance was written before God for those who love to worship and meditate on His name. Be mindful of this one thing, when we come to church and begin to worship God in spirit and in truth, every word that is spoken between us is recorded in the Book of Remembrance.

JUST TWO OR THREE

"For where two or three are gathered together in My name, I am there in the midst of them." (Matthew 18:20)

As we stated in a previous chapter, the original writing of this text reads like this, "Wherever there are two, there are three." When there are two or three, God is in the midst and establishes an atmosphere of glory. When God gets in the midst of it, He produces an environment for His glory to descend. When we are consciously aware of the true and living God, it is that awareness that brings us together on one accord. One can chase a thousand, but two can put ten thousand to flight.

If you are dealing with some very difficult situations in your life and there does not seem to be an answer, if you can come together with the one you're having a grievance with and allow the Holy Spirit to get in the midst, it will work out for your good. Are you a single parent in the midst of trying and difficult times? Hug your child and say, "Our breakthrough is on the way because God is in the midst." You don't have to fully understand everything, just cry out "Alleluia!" and watch the glory cloud show up.

"In the year that King Uzziah died, I saw the Lord sitting on a throne, high and lifted up, and the train of His robe filled the temple." (Isaiah 6:1)

Isaiah was having an out of body experience as he saw the Lord sitting on a throne and being lifted up. When did Isaiah have this revelation of the Lord? It was during the year that King Uzziah died. The reason why some saints can't see the glory of the Lord is because they have not died to their own strength. There is going to be an awesome revival in the earth when each saint, one-by-one, dies to self. You cannot truly see God until something dies. Most people have never had anything supernatural happen in their lives because everything that they depend upon is still there. It is not until a family member or close friend turns their back on them and they are left wounded and disappointed that you will look to the hills from whence comes their help.

If you have ever been hurt, you are a candidate for glory. If you have ever been disappointed, you are a candidate for glory. If you have ever been let down, backstabbed, bruised, messed up, wounded, wiped out or cut off, you are a perfect candidate for seeing God in a way that you have never seen Him before.

"And one cried to another and said: Holy, holy, holy [is] the LORD of hosts; the whole earth is full of His glory! And the posts of the door were shaken by the voice of him who cried out, and the

house was filled with smoke." (Isaiah 6:3-4)

I have come to the place in my worship experience where I now realize that I have not been using my mouth properly. I have been saying, "Lord, bless me." "Lord, do for me." The Holy Spirit said to me, "I dwell in the midst of a people of unclean lips." They have the utterance of tongues like the group Moses led out of Egypt -- "Lord, give me;" "Lord, help me;" "Lord, bless me;" "Lord, fix me." You hardly ever hear them saying, "Holy is thy name." "Worthy is the Lamb that was slain to receive glory and honor and power." I stood before God and said, "Make my lips clean!"

I heard God say, "My son, let the church know that every time they come to worship they should come looking to experience My glory. Heaven and earth are being filled with My glory. I am looking for a people that will demonstrate My love and My passion. Every time they cry out, "Holy, Holy, Holy," their lips are being cleansed. Every time they cry out, "Glory, wisdom, blessing and honor," their minds are being transformed into my likeness. This is what happens when you live with the glory of God.

CHAPTER 9

Experiencing The Riches Of His Glory

"Jesus therefore again groaning in himself cometh to the grave. It was a cave, and a stone lay upon it. Jesus said, Take ye away the stone. Martha, the sister of him that was dead, saith unto him, Lord, by this time he stinkett: for he hath been dead four days. Jesus saith unto her, Said I not unto thee, that, if thou wouldest believe, thou shouldest see the glory of God?" (John 11:38-40)

THE SEASON OF GLORY

It is time to let God be completely in charge of your life. This is the season of glory. God is pleased when we pursue His glory. Yet even more importantly, He wants us to understand that we cannot live without it. Living with the glory creates an environment for the miraculous. God is going to fully manifest Himself among believers with a wave of glory. We have been praying for it and we really want to see this wave. We therefore, have to create an environment that is conducive for glory every time we meet. We need an environment that is conducive for miracles. We need a 'glorious' environment that is lasting.

We must continue to fight to create this environment because breakthroughs, miracles and blessings come easily when glory is present. In that type of environment, we must expect God to bless and deliver His people. This is the season for glory. In short, we can strengthen our faith and expect anything and everything to occur.

Remember, you cannot get close to God without being blessed. You cannot stay in His presence long without being touched by His delivering hands. Any time God touches a people where His presence is, there is a supernatural flow. In that flow, we will experience the abundant life that He has already prepared for us.

When you live with the glory, God will take care of your every need. Our cry now does not have to be, "God, bless me, or God help me, or God fix me." Our cry should be, "God, release your glory. Cover me with your glory." When you are living under an open heaven and living with the glory of God, there is no lack in your life. God wants us to live with His glory every day and every night. Living with the glory means living without lack.

Some people have been living from paycheck to paycheck hoping that something extra would miraculously show up each day. The good news that I bring to you is to 'pursue the glory', learn how to live with it and watch God. Live with the glory and you will live without lack. You don't need money, you need His glory. Your greatest need is not a spouse or a house; what you really need is God's glory. When God comes with His glory, He brings with Him everything that He is.

"The mystery which has been hidden from ages and from generations, but now has been revealed to His saints. To them God willed to make known what are the riches of the glory of this mystery among the Gentiles: which is Christ in you, the hope of glory." (Colossians 1:26-27)

This mystery has been hidden from many for ages. The secret of how we need to cover ourselves and take care of our needs has been hidden from you for ages. Your great grandfather may have died poor. Your grandmother may have died struggling and satan thinks he is going to do the same thing with you by keeping you away from the knowledge of glory.

The scripture says, "The mystery which has been hidden from ages and from generations, but now has been revealed to His saints." The only way you cannot get excited about that is if you are not sure that you are a saint. The devil has been messing with you by telling you that you have to arrive at certain level of spirituality and that you do not qualify to become a Christian but the devil is a liar. If you are saved, you are a saint. According to the scripture, ages and generations of people have died and gone on without the knowledge of the glory. They have served God for years and have been faithful to Him, studied the Bible, taught the scriptures and preached messages with power but they did not come into the knowledge of the glory. Consequently, the mystery has been hidden from them but in this dispensation, the mystery is being revealed to the saints.

It is so heart-warming to know that you are a part of a generation to whom God is revealing knowledge that previous generations did not have the opportunity to receive. You have to be very careful, therefore, and take note of the fact that to whom much is given, much is required. (Luke 12:48)

Repeat after me, "I want to live with the glory of God. I am getting ready to see the mystery of the riches of the glory of God." Repeat these words until they penetrate your Spirit.

YOUR SHIELD OF PROTECTION

"LORD, how they have increased who trouble me! Many are they who rise up against me. Many are they who say of me, "There is no help for him in God." Selah. "But You, O LORD, are a shield for me ,my glory and the One who lifts up my head." (Psalm 3:1-3)

In verses 1-2, David is saying, when people get in their

private circles they are making a mockery about you and your God. They will say that you are talking about the power and the love of God but God has not done anything for you. The Lord is your shield and glory. Another word for shield is protection. "You, O Lord are a protection and the One who lifts up my head." All you have to do is hold on and watch God work on your behalf.

Your enemies may be great in number, but when you carry God's glory, you have the shield that cannot be broken. When you carry God's glory, you are protected. Whenever God puts a hedge or a shield of protection around you, He attaches glory and when that happens it also eliminates depression. You cannot carry God's glory and be depressed. In every situation, God's glory will make you lift up your head.

David said in Psalm 24, *"Lift up your heads O ye gates! Lift up your heads, ye everlasting doors!"* Why? "And the King of glory shall come in." You should get to the place in your life where you allow the King of glory to come in and take charge of your life. Allow the King of glory to take charge of your affairs, your marriage, your career, your family, your body. When the King of glory comes in, nothing else matters. You can be at peace and rest because the King has everything under control.

When glory comes, God lifts up your head! When glory comes, God builds up your self-esteem. When glory comes, your self-confidence gets boosted to another level and you feel like you can slay a giant. When glory comes, God restores your soul. David said, "The Lord is my Shepherd, I shall not want…. He restores my soul. He makes me lie down…." David must have had a taste of God's glory.

Let me take a moment to address those persons who have been having interrupted sleep or tormented rest. When you are asleep, you are in a state of unconsciousness and the devil has an opportunity to mess with your mind. But you do not have to worry, because you have a shield. You have a shield all around you and you can go to sleep in peace. You have a shield who is also your glory and the lifter-up of your head. If you have been tormented in recent times in your sleep and you have not been able to rest well, know that there is a shield of protection all around you. Rest! Trust God that He has everything under control and you can have sweet sleep.

God is our sun and shield. He is our light and our protection. He gives grace and glory. You cannot get God's glory without His grace, His unmerited favor. His glory automatically brings favor. When you have favor, you are positioned to receive what you do not deserve. When you have favor, you have access to areas that you are not qualified to go in. Glory! Favor! Glory! Favor! You do not have to pray for favor; just ask for God's glory. He gives glory and grace.

"For the LORD God is a sun and shield; the LORD will give grace and glory; no good thing will He withhold from those who walk uprightly." (Psalm 84:11)

The only thing that exempts you from the glory of favor

is an ungodly walk. Glory does not leave you, but favor will. The Lord will give grace and glory (favor and fame, favor and character, favor and authority, favor and power, favor and magnificence). No good thing (nothing) will He withhold from those who walk uprightly. When you walk uprightly with favor nothing good will God hold back from you, which means if you don't have it, then it isn't good for you now.

Now I fully understand the scripture where Jesus was talking to the multitudes and He said even the beasts of the field do not worry about anything. You don't need to worry just seek ye first the kingdom of God and His righteousness and then all of these things shall be added unto you. (Matthew 6:33) Too many Christians are losing because of worry. If you have the glory of God saturating your life then favor is on your life. If you want something and cannot get it then God has purposed to spare you and protect you from it for a reason. While some things are good for us, they may not be good now. We should not question God. We should just worship God, walk uprightly and watch God. You are under God's protection not only from other people but also from yourself. I hear God saying, "Whatever you need, if it is good for you, then I will give it to you. If I withhold it, then it is not good for you now." You cannot twist God's arms nor should you even try.

God promised that He will not withhold anything from you if you walk uprightly. So, if you want something and you do not have it, then there can only be one of two reasons -- either you have an ungodly walk and God has not shined His favor on your life, or you are walking uprightly and desiring something that is not good for you now. Wherever you are in your life right now, if your walk is upright, that is exactly where God wants you.

"Now a certain man was sick, Lazarus of Bethany, the town of Mary and her sister Martha. It was that Mary who anointed the Lord with fragrant oil and wiped His feet with her hair, whose brother Lazarus was sick. Therefore the sisters sent to Him, saying, "Lord, behold, he whom You love is sick." When Jesus heard that, He said, "This sickness is not unto death, but for the glory of God, that the Son of God may be glorified through it." (John 11:1-4)

Verse 5-6, "Now Jesus loved Martha and her sister and Lazarus. So, when He heard that he was sick, He stayed two more days in the place where He was." Jesus stayed two days longer. He concluded that He could not go to Lazarus right away because Lazarus and his family needed to go through that particular situation at that time. Jesus declared that his sickness was not unto death but for the glory of God, that the son of God may be glorified through it. God does not make you sick but God can use your illness as an opportunity for the world to see glory.

Jesus loved Lazarus, Mary and Martha, but instead of running to Lazarus' rescue, Jesus delayed His journey for two days. Jesus was saying, "I did not plan to stay here all this time, but I have to delay my journey, because if I go to Bethany, I know how I feel about Lazarus, I will heal him. But this is exactly where God wants Lazarus at this time. God does not want me to heal him.

God wants me to raise him." Do not worry about hardship, sickness or adverse situations that you may be going through. You had it before, and it is definitely worth repeating, God will turn the situation around for your good and for His glory.

"What if God, wanting to show His wrath and to make His power known, endured with much longsuffering the vessels of wrath prepared for destruction, and that He might make known the riches of His glory on the vessels of mercy, which He had prepared beforehand for glory. (Romans 9:22-23)

God knew you before you were formed in your mother's womb, and God knew where you would be and what you would be dealing with today. God has orchestrated the affairs of your life to make sure He gets the glory. Sometimes God will make known the riches of His glory, through the adversities that we experience in our lives. For those dealing with physical challenges in your bodies, if you are saved and you are walking uprightly, know that God really trusts you, because if He has positioned you beforehand for glory, God knows that you are not going to turn your back on Him. You may be having a 'Job' experience but remember Job's latter days were better than his former days. God will have the final say. Say this powerful affirmation to yourself, "I see glory coming from my life; my life will cause God to be glorified." Hold on and allow whatever it is to come full circle after you have suffered a while, you will obtain the prize.

CHAPTER 10

What To Expect When The Glory Comes

"For the earth will be filled with the knowledge of the glory of the LORD, as the waters cover the sea." (Habakkuk 2:14)

REVEALED GLORY

According to Isaiah 40:3-5, the glory of the Lord shall be revealed; and all flesh, whether they want to see it or not, will see it. Everyone may not bask in His glory, everyone may not benefit from it, but we will all see it. The whole earth will be filled with the glory of God, and all flesh shall see it together, for the mouth of the Lord has spoken it. God promised that the whole earth will be filled with His glory.

"This beginning of signs Jesus did in Cana of Galilee, and manifested His glory; and His disciples believed in Him." (John 2:11)

It wasn't until the glory was manifested that the disciples believed in Jesus. The people who He had called, people who were walking with Him, His armor bearers, the Bible says that it was not until His glory was manifested that they started to believe in Him. When they witnessed Jesus perform miracles, they believed.

There are people all over the world who will never believe in Jesus because we preach about His goodness. They want to see Him in all of His glory. They have heard enough preachers. They want to see what we preach manifested in our lives. They have observed that so much of what happens in the church is seasoned with a great degree of hypocrisy that they are no longer listening to the sermons. They want to see Jesus now, in all of His glory.

We are entering an appointed time on God's agenda. God is ready to reveal and establish His manifested presence in every region, in every country, in every city, on every island, in every church, and in every life. He wants to reveal and establish His manifested presence in our lives.

Some may say, "But Bishop, you don't know everything about me. If you really knew me, you would not say that He wants to reveal and establish His manifested presence in my life." No one is excluded from the list. He wants to reveal and establish His manifested presence in everyone's life, young and old. God wants to reveal and establish His manifested presence in the Caribbean, The Americas, Europe, Asia, India, Australia, Africa and all points in between.

God will shake the world no matter what it looks like. The nations will be shaken and some will experience God's wrath. God has been good to His people and has blessed us over the years but we have become a stiff-necked people. We have become a rebellious people. There are many people who have been blessed by God and will not even step into a church. They are out on their yachts fishing, playing golf, or on the basketball court. Some others are on the beaches using Sunday, the Lord's day, as a day of fun and frolic.

If our world does not change and go beyond serving God symbolically, God will remove His hand of blessings and only the people with the glory will know what it is to live in pleasure and with fullness of joy. There is coming a time real soon where you will notice that God's hand is either upon us or noticeably removed. There will be no gray area. The church of the living God is getting ready to witness a season in which God will open up the heavens and reveal Himself in the earth by the demonstration of His power and His glory.

As you are aware, the glory comes when there has been a collision between the earth realm and the heavenly realm, when the barrier between the two realms is removed from your life and

God steps out of His realm and moves into the earthly realm. When you see God show up like that in your life, you will be past days of going in the corner to cry because people hurt your feelings. You will be strong and very courageous because the glory also equips you for battle and gives you a strategic edge over the enemy. You will further realize that some things that used to be a mystery to you will no longer baffle you. When God's glory is revealed in your life, you will have lived to see the day when every tongue that rises up in judgment against you being condemned. Take my advice -- do not spend any more time trying to get revenge. Don't waste anymore of your time trying to get even with people who hurt your feelings or tried to damage your integrity. Wait for glory!

MIRACLES

Jesus never performed any miracles until His glory was manifested. When the glory was manifested, He performed a miracle and then His disciples believed in Him. As the people were celebrating at the wedding feast at Cana of Galilee, they ran out of wine. You remember Mary coming to Jesus and saying, "We have no more wine. You have to do something." Jesus responded to His mother and said, "My time has not yet come." Jesus did not know that glory had just been revealed. It took His mother to let Him know, "You can fix this." So, when Jesus said to His mother, "My time has not yet come," Mary went to the servant and said, "Whatever he tells you to do, do it." Then Jesus turned and said, "Fill up the water pots."

Soon you will see some things in the body of Christ beginning to dry up. Do not be alarmed. God has to do it so the people with glory can fill them back up. However, you cannot put new wine in old wineskins. When God dries up the pots. We are not just going to fill the pots, we must sanctify them first and new wine is going to be released in abundance. Whatever God tells you to do, do it.

Whenever Jesus touches your life, it is always for the better. When you see the glory manifested in your life, people will ask, "What did you do? What happened to you? Where have you been since I saw you last?" The glory of the Lord has risen upon me. The miracles that Jesus performed as He walked this earth were done, primarily, for the purpose of manifesting glory.

"Now as Jesus passed by, He saw a man who was blind from birth. And His disciples asked Him, saying, "Rabbi, who sinned, this man or his parents, that he was born blind?" Jesus answered, "Neither this man nor his parents sinned, but that the works of God should be revealed in him." (John 9:1-3)

Some people are living their lives with what they may regard as a defect, looking at their physical, tangible makeup in comparison to other people they admire, and they wonder why there are certain things they seemingly lack or why they have too much of certain things. God always does a perfect work. Whatever you regard as a defect was designed by God to bring Him glory and to reveal His good works.

SANCTUARY

Whenever the heavenly realm spills over into the earthly realm, all limitations are removed and anything is possible. So, stop fighting. Go for the glory. You don't have to wait for corporate glory to experience personal glory. You have to structure your life so that the realm of God can supersede the realm in which you live. You may see trials, you may see shortage, you may see dilemmas, but you will also see God, and God is bigger than whatever you see with your natural eye. God never sees shortage as shortage. God sees shortages as opportunities for miracles. God never sees defects as defects. God sees defects as opportunities to reveal His glory. God never sees problems as we may see them. God sees problems as opportunities for us to recognize that He is altogether lovely. When glory comes, all limitations are removed. It's time to go after the glory.

May the LORD answer you in the day of trouble; may the name of the God of Jacob defend you; may He send you help from the sanctuary, and strengthen you out of Zion; (Psalm 20:1-2)

"O God, You are my God; early will I seek You; my soul thirsts for You; my flesh longs for You in a dry and thirsty land where there is no water. So I have looked for You in the sanctuary, to see Your power and Your glory." (Psalm 63:1-2)

The above passages of scripture suggest that help is coming right from the sanctuary. When you come to the sanctuary you should come looking for God's power and God's glory. When you see His power, and see His glory, all the help you need you will get. Do you know why sick people are coming in the Lord's house and leaving sick? They worshipped without seeing God's power and God's glory. Do you know why people come in broken and leave fed up, discouraged, annoyed and unsaved? An environment has not been created for people to see God's power and God's glory.

The first Sunday after I came back from my time alone with the Lord, I said that all flesh has to get out of the way. Anyone standing in the way and trying to make themselves look big in our church had to step to the aside, because no flesh was going to glory in God's presence. When we come to the Lord's house we do not want to see people. We want to see God's power and His Glory. It does not matter what title or position you may hold. When we show up to worship, we must humble ourselves if we want to see God's power and His glory.

We have made the positions of men too significant in our churches. There are too many people in churches across this country and around the world who think that the church cannot go on without them. Jesus said, *"Upon this rock, I will build my church, and the gates of hell shall not prevail."* (Matthew 16:17) When a people belong to God, when hell comes against them, hell can only rock them, but hell cannot break them. We are a part of the Lord's church!

Blessings and breakthroughs come easily when God's glory is revealed. When God's glory is revealed, we will not have to do as much warfare in the spirit. We may have had to come against various demonic forces on occasion but when the glory of God is revealed, we will not have to do too much warfare on a consistent basis because breakthroughs and blessings come easily with God's glory. It is impossible to separate the glory of God from His power, His wisdom, His love, or His provision. When glory comes upon a people, everything that God has comes with it, His majesty, His splendor, His honor, His power, His authority, His wealth, His brilliance, His weight. I do not understand why any believer would want to live his/her life without the glory of God.

WHAT TO EXPECT!

When the glory of God is revealed, there are some things you can expect.

1. AN OVERWHELMING CONVICTION OF SIN

One of the things you can expect when the glory of God is revealed is *an overwhelming conviction of sin,* resulting in personal repentance. During the praise and worship time of our Sunday morning service at Mount Tabor, the Holy Spirit whispered in my ear, "Make an altar call right after praise and worship so that I can give you an indication of how close My glory is." I was obedient to the Holy Spirit and, without preaching, four people came to the altar for salvation and eight people came to rededicate their lives to God. Praise and worship ministries are going to be a vital part of this new dispensation of God's glory. If you are a part of a praise and worship team, God is saying, "Come up higher, because you are going to be partners with Me in this next season."

The first time we hear about God's glory in the Old Testament, God was telling Moses to take off his shoes, for the place He was standing was holy. (Exodus 3:5) God has connected holiness to glory. The Spirit of God is holy. When the glory of the Lord is revealed, un-holiness and unrighteousness will be exposed and expressed without embarrassment. Those who do not want to submit to the Lord's holiness and his righteous will be uncomfortable in His presence. They will either seek to get away from the environment of His glory or they will draw near to God and repent.

"In the year that King Uzziah died, I saw the Lord sitting on a throne, high and lifted up, and the train of His robe filled the temple. Above it stood seraphim; each one had six wings: with two he covered his face, with two he covered his feet, and with two he flew. And one cried to another and said: 'Holy, holy, holy is the LORD of hosts; the whole earth is full of His glory!' ⁴ *And the posts of the door were shaken by the voice of him who cried out, and the house was filled with smoke. So I said: 'Woe is me, for I am undone!   Because I am a man of unclean lips, and I dwell in the midst of a people of unclean lips; for my eyes have seen the King, the LORD of hosts.'"* (Isaiah 6:1-3)

When the glory of God was revealed, even the Prophet Isaiah started crying out, "Woe is me, for I am undone! I am a man of unclean lips, and I dwell in the midst of a people of unclean lips; for mine eyes have seen…" Until this divine revelation of the glory of God, I was preaching and prophesying but now that God's glory has been revealed, mine eyes have seen the King, and since I have seen the King, woe is me. You don't really see yourself until you see the King, and you don't see the King until you experience God's glory. When you see the King, you see yourself for who you really are; and most of us, when we see ourselves for who we really are, will have to throw our hands up and say, "Woe is me!"

When the glory was revealed to the Prophet Isaiah, he saw himself and he said, "Woe, this is me?" In other words, "I can't believe what I am looking at! "Woe is me! I am undone. I don't qualify for what I just received because my lips are dirty, and I dwell with a bunch of people with dirty lips. But I have seen the King and because I have seen the King, I cannot stay like this." Isaiah was repenting.

Let's look at Psalm 51:7. *"Purge me with hyssop, and I shall be clean; wash me, and I shall be whiter than snow."* David, a man after God's own heart, and God's choice said, "Purge me with hyssop and I shall be clean." That means, "I am dirty now, but if you purge me, I will be clean." "Wash me and I will be whiter than snow."

Verse 8-9, *"Make me hear joy and gladness, that the bones You have broken may rejoice. Hide Your face from my sins, and blot out all my iniquities."* Wipe out all my iniquities, all my filth, all my junk, take it out. I see God's glory, so I cannot stay in this state.

Verses 10-13, "Create in me a clean heart, O God, and renew a steadfast spirit within me. Do not cast me away from Your presence, and do not take Your Holy Spirit from me." Restore to me the joy of Your salvation, and uphold me by Your generous Spirit. Then I will teach transgressors Your ways, and sinners shall be converted to You."

When God's glory is revealed in your life, you have to ask Him to create in you a clean heart and to renew the right Spirit within you. "This heart that I have, I can't make it with this. Now that your glory is revealed in my life, I don't even want you to fix this one; just take it out."

The glory of God is so heavy that you cannot carry it and carry your sins. That is too much weight. We are getting ready to witness the evolution of a church where pastors, ministers, elders, evangelists, servants, and leaders will say, "Jesus, I have sinned. Wash me. Cleanse me." I am talking about people from the pews to the pulpit, at all levels of the church recommitting to a life of holiness. It will be difficult for people to sneak and serve any more because once you enter into the House of God, the glory of the Lord will be too heavy to entertain that kind of hypocrisy and the weight of your sin. We are about to witness people running to the altar in the middle of the sermon, falling on their knees in surrender. We won't know what they are saying to God but between them and God, they are working out their sins and trying to reclaim the joy of their salvation.

God says, "Since the preaching of the gospel is not affecting you then, I'll get your attention with my glory because I can't afford to lose you." I hear God saying, "There is a heavy anointing on His people for national service to the kingdom. I cannot afford to let you knock yourself out of the race because of sin." When God's glory is poured out upon an individual's life, on a church, on a city or on a nation, sin is exposed and repentance breaks forth. Righteousness exalts a nation. Sin is a reproach to any people.

"What shall we say then? Shall we continue in sin that grace may abound? (Romans 6:1)

Verse 12, *"Therefore do not let sin reign in your mortal body, that you should obey it in its lusts."*

Verse 14, *"For sin shall not have dominion over you, for you are not under law but under grace."*

I am confident that the glory of God is getting ready to descend upon us very soon. When the glory impacts your life, sin will no longer have dominion over you. Every time sin tries to come in, it will have to leave. It will not be able to take residence. Every time it tries to take root, it will be uprooted. Sin will no longer have dominion over you.

The body of Christ is getting ready to see repentance erupt everywhere. If you are going to become a carrier of the glory, then wherever you go repentance has to break forth uncovering sins hidden for years. We will see old people, middle-aged people and young people throwing up their hands and saying, "God I repent! Wash me. Purge me. Create in me a clean heart, Lord.

2. A GREAT SENSE OF PEACE AND SECURITY

When the glory of God is revealed in the lives of God's people, *you can expect to see people filled with a great sense of peace and security.* The weight of worry and concern will be lifted. You may have bills to pay, challenges with your health, family or on your job but God's glory allows you to be at peace. In an environment of glory you will remember the times when God delivered you in the past.   Jesus Christ is the same yesterday, today and forever. When the glory of God is manifested in your life, you will feel the peace of God flooding your heart. Problems look much smaller in the face of His glory.

The peace of God carries a cleansing dimension and we feel clean and forgiven in the presence of God, not filthy and unworthy. The Holy Spirit will bear witness in your heart that you are a child of God forgiven.

"For thus says the LORD of hosts: 'Once more (it is a little while) I will shake heaven and earth, the sea and dry land; and I will shake all nations, and they shall come to the Desire of All Nations, and I will fill this temple with glory,' says the LORD of hosts. 'The silver is Mine, and the gold is Mine,' says the LORD of hosts. 'The glory of this latter temple shall be greater than the former,' says the LORD of hosts. 'And in this place I will give peace,' says the LORD of hosts." (Haggai 2:6-9)

God says, "I will shake all nations!" This House of God will be filled with His glory when He shakes the nations and He will give peace to His house. Companies are downsizing and governments laying off employees because God is getting ready to shake the world.

We did not really need this shaking. All we had to do was stay with God but we made a wrong turn. When He shakes us, He will fill the house with glory and only if you are in the House, you will experience the glory. The peace of God will surpass all human understanding and people will wonder how you can be so calm in the midst of the storm. It is because of the glory.

I am convinced that God is about to re-establish His presence once again in the nations. The Lord God Almighty, Jehovah is Lord over the nations. Our God reigns! Therefore, the witches will not have the last word over our marriages. The enemy will not be able to upset our lives and turn them upside down. When glory comes the world will know that our God reigns.

"Be anxious for nothing, but in everything by prayer and supplication, with thanksgiving, let your requests be made known to God; and the peace of God, which surpasses all understanding, will guard your hearts and minds through Christ Jesus." (Philippians 4:6-7)

The spirit of thanksgiving will cause the peace of God to guard your heart. You don't thank Him for everything; You thank Him in all things.

3. PEOPLE FILLED WITH THE JOY OF THE LORD

When the glory of the Lord is revealed, *expect to see evidence of people filled with the joy of the Lord.* When the glory of the Lord is manifested in the House of God, there will be people during Sunday morning worship who will be filled with the joy of the Lord in the middle of service, with no natural explanation. They will experience a holy laughter. They may not know why they are laughing, but they will not be able to stop laughing. However, it will be a laughter without disturbance.

"You will show me the path of life; in Your presence is fullness of joy; at Your right hand are pleasures forevermore." (Psalm 16:11)

You will see people who are behind in their mortgage, car payments and other bills, yet filled with joy and talking about the goodness of God. Those who really experience the manifested glory of God in their lives will not describe God as merely blessing them. They will say, "When I think about the goodness of Jesus and all He has done for mc, I can dance." There will be a reawakening to the realization that this joy you have, 'the world didn't give it and the world can't take it away'.

"For the kingdom of God is not eating and drinking, but righteousness and peace and joy in the Holy Spirit." (Romans 14:17)

You cannot manufacture righteousness, and peace and joy in your church. You cannot orchestrate it. It has to be righteousness, peace and joy in the Holy Ghost. This joy will be so great that it will be almost symbolic of the exuberance that filled the lives of the people on the day of Pentecost. When the glory of the

Lord fell on the 120 persons gathered in the Upper Room, the skeptics accused them, saying, "You fellas are drunk, filled with wine." Peter responded by saying, "Yes, we are drunk, but not as you suppose; but this is that which was spoken by the Prophet Joel."

When the glory and the joy of the Lord is manifested in your midst, you and those around you will be affected; your children, your friends and your housekeeper. When the glory of God is revealed, if your niece is living in your house, she will experience it; if your nephew lives with you, he will experience it.

I am putting my prophetic anointing on the line, I heard the Lord say that when the glory of God begins to fall schools, neighborhoods, cities, states, and regions will take a turn. Instead of violence, bad grades and sexual promiscuity, we will see revival breaking out at schools. I see the Spirit of God descending upon our schools. We will see parents being called to the school and told, "We need pastors and counselors to come into these schools because children are slain in the Holy Ghost. We need some spiritual people to come help us make some sense out of all that is happening."

4. UNCONTROLLABLE WEEPING

When the Glory of the Lord is revealed, *you can expect to see people with uncontrollable weeping,* weeping caused by either sorrow over sin or because the fullness of joy that they have found in the presence of God has overwhelmed them.

Some people will feel tormented because they have sinned against God, which will cause them to weep. When God's glory is manifested in your life, it is difficult to be entangled in sin without a guilty conscience. When the Holy Spirit invades your environment, sin has to be exposed and expressed. So, you will see people weeping. You will not need to give them tissue; they are in sorrow over sin. Give them space to weep but if they are sitting in their pew just weeping, if you are spiritual, stretch your hands toward them and say, "Lord, cover them right now, in Jesus' name. Let everything wrong be fixed." Do not disturb their sorrow. Allow them to stay there and weep and work it out with God.

There will be some people crying at the altar because they are overwhelmed with the fact that God has considered them worthy of His glory. Some people may say, "Hallelujah," others will weep, still others will run. God does not move everybody in the same way. You will see uncontrollable weeping, but it will not just be a weeping. Here is how you can distinguish the sound. You will hear people weeping, and some of them, literally, in their weeping will produce a sound that carries the flavor of prayer, a sound that will push you to prayer because the prayers of the righteous availeth much.

The spirit of repentance will overtake the people and they will turn to God with weeping, fasting and mourning. Some will fast, others will weep, still others will mourn. We have lost the Spirit of travail in the body of Christ. We used to mourn before we had money; we used to mourn before we had big houses, a couple of cars and nice clothes. We were used to people travailing at the altar, nowadays that has become a rare occurrence.

"Blow the trumpet in Zion, consecrate a fast, call a sacred assembly; gather the people, sanctify the congregation, assemble the elders, gather the children and nursing babes; let the bridegroom go out from his chamber, and the bride from her dressing room. Let the priests, who minister to the LORD. Weep between the porch and the altar; let them say, "Spare Your people, O LORD, and do not give Your heritage to reproach, that the nations should rule over them. Why should they say among the peoples, 'Where is their God?'" (Joel 2:15-17)

Our nations have turned their backs on God. We have been so blessed that we are becoming victims of our blessings. Those of us who occupy the pulpit, our major job is to blow the trumpet in Zion, consecrate ourselves, fast, call a sacred assembly, gather the people, sanctify the congregation, (that's our job) assemble the elders, gather the children and nursing babes.

If we are serious about God's glory and serious about our assignment from God, we must find time outside of regular worship to get before the altar and weep before God. My job is to blow the trumpet, to sound the alarm. I have to call people out of sin. Some may not like me in this season because I have to call them out of sin. We have to finally get to the point where we can raise up at least one church in every city where sinners can begin to look at some of us and say, "I better stay away from there because if I go near them, God will touch my life."

As believers, we have to sanctify ourselves. Sanctification is not a denomination. Every believer is supposed to walk with a level of sanctification. Many believers like to talk about grace, often quoting, "His grace is sufficient." Many think that means you can live a low life and God's grace is sufficient. No! There is a level of sanctification that we have all been called into as believers, and it is my job to make sure that people are knowledgeable about sanctification, and are convicted if they do not walk in sanctification.

Many Christians have it too easy. There is no accountability. They feel they can do whatever they want to do. However, that is not the kingdom way. There is a King and then there are subjects. God expects us to walk in righteousness. At some point, we have to raise up a people with whom God is pleased. We have to start making people accountable for their actions. If you want to be on the praise and worship team, people should be able to sense the glory of God on your life. Preachers, deacons, servants and elders must be accountable. If you say you are a preacher, then let your lifestyle reflect your calling.

Ushers should be holy, protocol people should be sanctified, public relations people should know Jesus, technical people should know a sound in the Spirit so they can produce a good sound in the building. We should call everyone into account. Your life should be an open book. Elders of our churches should be holy men and women of God. We do not need to have elders laying hands on people and they have filthy, lives because spirits transfer. You should not want an ungodly bishop blessing you when you come to the altar for a blessing over your life, your marriage or your career.

We have reached the point where we have to hold more than the bishop accountable. We have to hold everyone in leadership and everyone in the congregation accountable. We cannot have musicians who just play well. We need musicians who are holy, righteous and sanctified. Everyone has to be accountable.

In this season of glory, every pastor, every preacher, every servant, every leader, every married member has to fight for their marriage, no matter the obstacle. Everybody who is married has issues. It does not matter how perfect you think your marriage is, we all have something in our marriage to work on. You cannot let the glory come upon you and then be quick to walk away from your marriage. Stand still and see the salvation of the Lord.

God never turned His back on you. He promised that He will supply all of your needs, according to His riches in glory. That means if you need healing, God has to manifest it; if you need finances, God has to supply; if you need friendships, God has to supply; if you need a husband or a wife, God's has to supply. David said, *"God is our refuge and strength, a very present help in trouble. (Psalm 46:1). Though an host should encamp against me, my heart shall not fear: though war should rise against me, in this will I be confident. One thing have I desired of the LORD, that will I seek after; that I may dwell in the house of the LORD all the days of my life, to behold the beauty of the LORD, and to enquire in his temple."* (Psalm 27:3-4).

5. EVIDENCE OF PHYSICAL WEAKNESS

When the glory comes, *you can expect to see evidence of physical weakness.* Periodically, people will be unable to stand in the presence of God, because they will be captivated by the power of God. Some theologians call it becoming "drunk in the spirit." You have heard of the phrase in 1 Corinthians, the "weight of glory." When you experience the weight of God's glory people may not be able to stand in His presence for a long period of time because it is so heavy.

There are stages of glory. The scripture says that we go from glory, to glory, to glory, to glory. Some people will be able to take it, and some people will not be able to stand it. Glory will hit you on different levels. Some may get an ounce of it at one time, some may get a pound, some may get three pounds, some may get four ounces, while some may get 20 pounds because of the weight of glory at times. You cannot stand up under it.

Some of you will be slain in the Spirit. You may be in your own personal devotion time when the weight of His glory takes control. The glory will not bring embarrassment to you. God is not out to embarrass you. He will rebuke you first. Glory comes in different portions.

John 18 verses 1-6, *"When Jesus had spoken these words, He went out with His disciples over the Brook Kidron, where there was a garden, which He and His disciples entered." "And Judas, who betrayed Him, also knew the place; for Jesus often met there with His disciples. Then Judas, having received a detachment of troops, and officers from the chief priests and Pharisees, came there with lanterns, torches and weapons. Jesus therefore, knowing all things that would come upon Him, went forward and said to them, 'Whom are you seeking?' They answered Him, Jesus of Nazareth; Jesus said to them, 'I am He.' And Judas, who betrayed Him, also stood with them. Now when He said to them, 'I am He,' they drew back and fell to the ground."*

When the people who came to arrest Jesus realized that they were in the presence of Jesus, they fell to the ground. Sometimes that is what will happen to us in the presence of God.

Acts 9:3-4 says, *"As he journeyed he came near Damascus, and suddenly a light shone around him from heaven. Then he fell to the ground, and heard a voice saying to him, "Saul, Saul, why are you persecuting Me?"* When the glory of God shone in and around Saul, his assignment changed. He fell from his horse straight to the ground. You don't have to be standing. You could be sitting and fall under the presence of God or the weight of His glory may rest upon your shoulders pushing you to move forward. We have to understand the glory of God and the reaction to the glory of God and signals and signs that follow the manifested and revealed presence of God through His glory. It is nothing that we need to fear; it is nothing of which we need to be ashamed. We cannot be reluctant to flow with every expression of the presence of His glory.

The Lord wants to tell you something in secret. Sometimes

when the glory of the Lord comes as a result of the manifested revealed presence of God, you have an opportunity to get a rhema word from God. Sometimes God will speak through the preacher, through the proclaimed word of God. But there are other times when God wants to say something directly to you, and He will give you a personal revelation.

"And when I saw Him, I fell at His feet as dead. But He laid His right hand on me, saying to me, "Do not be afraid; I am the First and the Last." (Revelation 1:17)

John is describing his experience and says he was slain in the Spirit. By the time John got up, he was no longer afraid of those people who wanted to banish him. You must understand where John was when he saw this in the Spirit. John was on the island of Patmos, where they were getting ready to boil him for preaching the gospel. They took John to the isle of Patmos and said this is where we are going to cut you off from preaching the gospel. As they were getting ready to boil him, he was slain in the Spirit. They couldn't touch him. They thought he was already dead.

Sometimes God may bring you to church and slay you in the Spirit because He is protecting you from something. Sometimes the weight of God's glory will create a state of physical weakness. Sometimes when God wants to get our attention so that He can reveal His divine wisdom, He has to take full control but some people have a need to be in control at all times. They have to be able to figure out everything and sometimes everything does not always make sense.

6. INTENSIFIED WORSHIP

When the Glory comes, you can expect the worship to be intensified. You have to tune your ear to hear new worship music being birthed in the midst of worship. You have to be cognizant of musicians creating their own music in service while they are in the presence of the Lord. You have to expect unrehearsed worship to break out suddenly in the House. There is an inseparable link between worship and the glory of God.

Worship brings God's presence into manifestation. Once the glory of God manifests it produces worship in the hearts of those present who genuinely love the Lord. When the glory of God saturates the House, it is going to be difficult for anyone who really loves God to sit idly by and watch without participating. Worship will break out! The realm of heaven spills into the earth realm through His glory. Worship is continual in heaven and it is responded to in like manner by those in the earth.

"After these things I looked, and behold, a door standing open in heaven. And the first voice which I heard was like a trumpet speaking with me, saying, "Come up here, and I will show you things which must take place after this." (Revelation 4:1)

That is what God is saying to some of us now. That is why it is important for you to clear your spirit and your mind. Get rid of the junk and the garbage in your life and in your spirit because God is calling you higher. God said, "I want you to come up higher and when you come up higher I will show you things which must take place after this." God is saying, "I want you to come up from the level that you are on because I want to show you what is to come."

I don't have the level of tolerance I used to have at one time, because I see God's glory coming. Glory is supposed to hit the body of Christ shortly. It is supposed to hit the whole body. Now, while everyone may not experience His glory at one time, no one is supposed to contaminate it. We cannot have the glory of God contaminated. There are more people who want God's glory than those who do not want His glory. There are more people in the Body who want to protect God's glory. So, let those of us who want it saturate our churches and communities with His glory and do all that we can to usher in His manifested presence.

God's glory does not come easy, nor is it free. It is time to cry out "Holy!" I don't want to go into the glory with anything hindering my mind or my spirit because the weight of His glory is enough to carry. Every once in a while you may slip and fall short of the glory of God, but you cannot live your life committing sin that was planned, arranged and pre-orchestrated.

We don't look to man, who will be with you today and shift on you tomorrow. We serve a God who changes not. He is the same yesterday, today and forever! He is all together Lovely! He is a Wonderful Counselor, the Mighty God, the Everlasting Father, the Prince of Peace! He is the Joy of my Salvation! That is where I get my joy from. I don't need anyone to crank me up to make me happy. I get joy in knowing that Jesus is mine.

Holy, Holy, Holy! Heaven and earth are full of your glory. The Bible says, "Whenever the living creatures give glory and honor and thanks to Him who sits on the throne, who lives forever and ever, the twenty-four elders fall down before Him who sits on the throne and worship Him who lives forever and ever, and cast their crowns before the throne, saying: *'You are worthy, O Lord, To receive glory and honor and power, For You created all things, And by Your will they exist and were created."* (Revelation 4:9-11)

Every time you worship God, you activate the twenty-four elders in glory. Let's take a look at where they are situated. They are around the throne, which is where God sits. Do you know why the devil does not want you to worship? Do you know why the devil will make you tired and weary and sleepy in church? Every time you go to worship, the twenty-four elders start bowing before God saying Holy, Holy, Holy. "I see My child down there worshipping God, so open up the gate and let him come into your presence." These elders represent intercessors in heaven. They go before God and they begin to move God. They go on your behalf and just start bowing and worshipping, crying, "Holy, Holy, Holy, Lord God Almighty, who was and is and is to come. There goes another one. She is crying out to you Lord. You have not given us the power to understand what she is crying out to you for, but You know all things. So, right now Lord, we come in agreement in heaven with your child's worship on earth. You said whatever we bind on earth, shall be bound in heaven."

Undoubtedly, it will always be a fight to worship. Worship is not an easy thing to do, because the rewards are so great. Every time I enter into worship, I activate the twenty-four elders in heaven.

7. UNUSUAL SIGNS AND WONDERS

When the Glory comes, you can expect to see unusual signs and wonders. You can expect to see signs that would make people wonder. God will use people to make the signs and cause people to wonder. They will include miracles, healings and unprecedented demonstrations of God's power. Don't expect to simply see the events that are outlined in the Bible repeated. In this dispensation, God intends to exceed what He has already done among men. God loves out-doing Himself because we serve a progressive God.

Let's observe Jeremiah 33:1-3.

"Moreover the word of the LORD came to Jeremiah a second time, while he was still shut up in the court of the prison, saying, "Thus says the LORD who made it, the LORD who formed it to establish it (the LORD is His name): 'Call to Me, and I will answer you, and show you great and mighty things, which you do not know.'" (Jeremiah 33:1-3)

I believe that this is exactly where we will be as believers when the glory of God hits segments of the body of Christ. Even before the whole earth is filled with His glory, believers will be able to call out to God and He will show them great and mighty things that they know not of.

Let's look at Acts 19:11-12.

"Now God worked unusual miracles by the hands of Paul, so that even handkerchiefs or aprons were brought from his body to the sick, and the diseases left them and the evil spirits went out of them."

Warning: The church is not to seek after signs and wonders, but we should not be surprised when unusual things are experienced.

In the book of Exodus, we see that God's abiding presence had been hovering over the people by a pillar of cloud by day and a pillar of fire by night.

- Water had been flowing from a rock;
- Bread (manna) had been falling out of the sky;
- All the people were delivered from their diseases.

Signs and wonders from God are nothing new. But when the glory of God hits a people, expect that people will experience unusual signs and wonder.

8. PEOPLE LOSING AN AWARENESS OF TIME WHEN IN HIS PRESENCE

When the glory of God hits a congregation and that congregation makes an effort to protect the glory, they will have no problem getting people to church. The problem will be getting them to leave.

- Whenever the Super Bowl goes into overtime, no one complains.
- Whenever an NBA game goes into overtime, no one complains.
- Whenever the World Series goes into extra innings, no one complains.

However, when church services go longer than expected, people usually complain.

When the glory of God hits a people, you can expect to see many of God's people going into overtime. You can expect to see them going into extra innings. People will not be eager to come out of the manifested presence of God. I remember when the glory of God first touched down in Mount Tabor people attending our 10:00 a.m. service did not begin to leave until 4:30 p.m. that afternoon.

Moses was lost in the presence of the glory of God for forty days and nights. There is something about being in the presence of God. You can expect to see people staying in the sanctuary long after the benediction has been given because they simply do not want to leave the glory that was lingering in the sanctuary.

9. DREAMS AND VISION

When the glory comes, you can expect to hear of an unusual number of people seeing visions and dreaming dreams.

Let's observe Ezekiel 1:1

"Now it came to pass in the thirtieth year, in the fourth month, on the fifth day of the month, as I was among the captives by the River Chebar, that the heavens were opened and I saw visions of God."

Now take note of Acts 10:10-11

"Then he became very hungry and wanted to eat; but while they made ready, he fell into a trance and saw heaven open and an object like a great sheet bound at the four corners, descending to him and let down to the earth."

In an earlier chapter we looked at Revelation 1:10-11. Let's look at it again.

"I was in the Spirit on the Lord's Day, and I heard behind me a loud voice, as of a trumpet, saying, "I am the Alpha and the Omega, the First and the Last," and, "what you see, write in a book and send it to the seven churches which are in Asia: to Ephesus, to Smyrna, to Pergamos, to Thyatira, to Sardis, to Philadelphia, and to Laodicea."

There is a dimension of the prophetic that can only come forth in the realm of God's glory. The more of the glory of God that is experienced, the more the voice of God will be heard and visions will be seen.

In Joel 2:28-29 we see these words:

"And it shall come to pass afterward that I will pour out My

Spirit on all flesh; your sons and your daughters shall prophesy, your old men shall dream dreams, your young men shall see visions. And also on My menservants and on My maidservants I will pour out My Spirit in those days."

I believe this passage speaks of the post-glory days. We are entering an appointed time on God's agenda. God wants to reveal and establish His manifested presence in every region, country, island, city, church and life. The church of the living God is getting ready to witness a season in which God will open up the heavens and reveal Himself in the earth by the great demonstrations of His power and His glory.

CHAPTER 11

Preparation for the Glory

Let me begin this portion by emphasizing the fact that unfortunately, most Christians do not like to pray. However, prayer is an integral part of experiencing God's glory. Here are three reasons why many Christians do not like to pray.

1. Many Christians do not like to pray because they lack the desire to fellowship with God. They are really not that excited about their relationship with the Lord. As a result, they lack the desire to have fellowship with the Lord.

2. Many Christians do not like to pray because they lack discipline in their own lives to pray. A strong prayer life demands discipline.

3. Many Christians do not like to pray because they think

they need to sound like the pastor, which gives them the false impression that praying is easy.

Praying may look easy, but developing a prayer life is difficult. The person who does not have a prayer life will not feel the desire to pray. They may pray when it is convenient or if they are asked to pray. They may pray when they are in a jam; they may pray when they want to bless a meal; they may pray before they go to bed or pray when they first get up, or they may pray when they are in trouble but that is not necessarily developing a prayer life.

HE'S IN THE MIDST

"For where two or three are gathered together in my name, there am I in the midst of them." (Matthew 18:20)

The original translation of Matthew 18:20 says, "Wherever there are two, there are three." You do not need a crowd to experience God's glory. Husbands and wives can create glory in their homes because wherever there are two coming together in His name, there are three. God says, "Wherever I see two people coming together in my name, there am I. My presence is right there, and I will create for them an environment for my glory to dwell."

Prayer partners are instrumental in building the kingdom. However, it is not the function of prayer partners to discuss other people's business. Prayer partners come together for the sake of having two people touching in the name of Jesus. It is not the prayer partners' function to prophesy. I don't need my prayer partners to shift their focus from touching and agreeing in His name, to being my theologian. That is not the order of God, and He will not be the third person in the midst in those settings. He is a God of order. Remember, wherever there are two, there are three.

After reading this book, single mothers should no longer be complaining because wherever there are two, there are three. The scripture did not say wherever there are two or three righteous people or two or three saved people, or two or three holy and sanctified people. The scripture clearly says, "Where two or three are gathered..." I can find a drunkard if I am in trouble and say, "Let's call on Jesus." All you need is for someone to come in agreement with the name of Jesus and God is instantly in the midst. That is good news!

So for the single mothers who are struggling and do not know where to turn, I can tell you where to turn. Turn to your child. She may be only six years-old but can she understand? That's all you need. Grab your child's hand and the two of you come together in agreement and call on the name of Jesus. Say, "Look here, baby, mommy is having a struggle buying groceries and paying the rent, gas, electric and telephone bills. I need God to come through and do something for me." Your little child may not know what she is doing but she does not have to. You have to know. You are only using the child to touch and agree so that the third person (God) can show up in the midst. The child is only a number because where two or three are gathered, God is truly in the midst and His glory is present and available.

RIGHT POSTURE

Many Christians go to God begging, and as a result they become discouraged because they don't see their prayers being answered. Think about this for a moment. If begging during prayer actually released God's favor in your life, then everyday you would beg. Your mind would start thinking, "If I beg today, I will get tomorrow." Thank God, He does not operate in that manner. The Apostle Paul says, "God has made us a promise that He shall supply our needs." God does not expect us to spend a lot of time talking about our needs during prayer.

God said, "I have made a commitment and promise to you that I will supply all of your needs according to My riches in Christ Jesus." Get it right with Jesus and let Him intercede on your behalf. God has breathed the breath of His Spirit into your life. When you approach God the right way, He is able to do exceedingly, abundantly above all you could ever ask or perceive. What most people are asking God for, they can handle themselves! Think about your own life and imagine if the only reason why you were the most popular person on campus was a result of always giving when your friends would ask for something. How would it make you feel to know that they were not in the relationship for love just what they can get out of it?

As we prepare for the coming wave of glory that is about to sweep over the church, our prayer posture is going to be significant. Start preparing right now by getting into a prayer mode that is going to force you to stay focused on the things of God while praying. Keep this in mind. Any time you find yourself praying for your needs over the needs of someone else, and the work of the kingdom, you have gone off course.

Jesus said, "When you pray, say…" And when you have finished saying, you must go back and read the word of God to see what God is saying back to you. God will not tell you anything new that He has not already told you in the Bible. Sometimes it is just a matter of discerning what He is saying so that you can understand the rhema (or the spoken) word of God. The Bible represents the logos word of God. However, at a particular time in your life when God speaks to you and an extraction from the word of God becomes relevant to your personal situation, that makes the logos word rhema in your life. But you have to "say" it to see. You could read the Bible and not understand anything you read but when you talk to God, and you read the Bible to hear Him talk back to you then the Holy Spirit helps you to understand what before seemed like a foreign language.

HEAVENLY PRAYER LANGUAGE

"The four living creatures, each having six wings, were full of eyes around and within. And they do not rest day or night, saying: "Holy, holy, holy, Lord God Almighty, Who was and is and is to come!" (Revelation 4:8)

The enemy of your soul will not want you to fully grasp what you are reading because if you should ever open your mouth and start giving God His glory, it will cause the 24 elders to fall down before Him. I believe that now more than ever before, believers of God must start opening up their mouths and using their heavenly prayer language to create an atmosphere to receive the blessings of God. Once the atmosphere is conductive to receive His glory, the heavens will open for you. It is absolutely impossible to live with God's glory and not see the blessings of God. God wants me to remind you that He is here to stay, so you might as well start giving Him praise with your mouth.

The proper attitude for worship is, "I will bless you, oh Lord; I will bless you, oh Lord; With my hands lifted up and my mouth filled with praise, with a heart of thanksgiving, I will bless you, oh Lord." Our highest calling in prayer is not to get from God, but simply to meet God in His sanctuary. When this becomes our attitude, our prayer life is going to excel. When God begins to anticipate you meeting with Him by entering into His sanctuary with a pure and open heart, I believe it brings a smile to His face.

God who is omniscient, the Alpha and Omega, knows what you will need tomorrow and a month from now. The church must be willing to make a total turnaround from where we are now to where God is taking us. If only fifty percent of the church would adjust their attitudes toward prayer, I truly believe that the rest will follow.

THE SECRET PLACE

"He that dwelleth in the secret place of the most High shall abide under the shadow of the Almighty." (Psalm 91:1)

In the presence of God all things become possible, if we believe and trust in Him. Let's look at the present economy. From a bad housing market to an unstable job market, the economists are selling us gloom and doom, then they say trust your government. You can only trust God and God alone! The body of Christ should not be worrying about what we should eat or where we should sleep because we are dwelling in the secret place of the most High.

How does one enter into the secret place of the most high? Remember Peter and John were on their way to the temple and they saw the lame man at the Gate Beautiful and Peter said, "Silver and Gold have I not, but what I have I give freely in the name of Jesus. Now rise up and walk." The man got up and started walking. He didn't walk because Peter told him to walk. It was the glory resting on him that caused the lame man to walk. During economic turbulence the voice of God is going to fall on His children who are lame and unable to walk, because they have become crippled by the system. When the glory falls, a loud voice will be heard all across the land that says, "Get up and start walking into your divine son/daughtership."

God rewards those who diligently seek Him, which means going after Him with a passion. This happens in your prayer time and in your worship time. You must go after Him. You must have a longing to be with Him. Once you have a taste of His Glory and once you have been in His presence, you look forward to returning there. King David said it best when he said, *"One thing have I desired of the LORD, that will I seek after; that I may dwell in the house of the LORD all the days of my life, to behold the beauty of the LORD, and to enquire in his temple."* (Psalm 27:4)

King David understood that in his day the temple was the abiding place for the presence of God. When King David was talking about being in the temple, he was referring to being in the presence of God and experiencing his glory.

"But the hour cometh, and now is, when the true worshippers shall worship the Father in spirit and in truth: for the Father seeketh such to worship him." (John 4:23)

The writer went from the present continuous tense to the present tense by saying the hour is coming and is now. The Holy Spirit wants to work something miraculous in your life, not in a year, not in a week, but right now. There are doors being forced open for you just because you are a worshipper. God is looking for people who will worship Him in spirit and in truth, those who are not afraid to meet Him face-to-face. This kind of relationship produces love at first sight. When two or three gather in His midst there will be an amazing experience in the heavenly realm and the earth realm. I hear the people of God singing and shouting because full restoration is coming to the House of the Lord.

Jesus taught us how to pray, "Our Father, who art in heaven, hallowed be thy name." When you pray, the first thing you must do is acknowledge the prayer giver. Let God know that He is the reason why you are praying. With this attitude toward prayer you cannot help but to offer up to God thanksgiving for what He is doing in your life. The more you thank God, the closer you get to Him. Spirit of the Living God, fall a fresh on me!

"And he said unto them, when ye pray, say, Our Father which art in heaven, Hallowed be thy name. Thy kingdom come. Thy will be done, as in heaven, so in earth." (Luke 11:2)

Pneuma Life Publishing
12138 Central Ave
Mitchellville, MD 20721
www.pneumalife.com
For bulk purchases call: 1-800-727-3218

Neil Ellis Ministries
E-mail: info@neilellisministries.com

Bahamas Address
Mt. Tabor Drive
P.O. Box N-9705
Nassau, Bahamas
1-242-392-0708

USA Address
3405 N.W. 189th St.
Miami Gardens, FL 33056-2907
Toll Free 1 (888) 700-FIRE